# Mastering Git and GitHub for Version Control

## Learn to Manage, Collaborate, and Deploy Code Like a Pro

**Greyson Chesterfield**

# COPYRIGHT

# DISCLAIMER

The information provided in this book is for general informational purposes only. All content in this book reflects the author's views and is based on their research, knowledge, and experiences. The author and publisher make no representations or warranties of any kind concerning the completeness, accuracy, reliability, suitability, or availability of the information contained herein.

This book is not intended to be a substitute for professional advice, diagnosis, or treatment. Readers should seek professional advice for any specific concerns or conditions. The author and publisher disclaim any liability or responsibility for any direct, indirect, incidental, or consequential loss or damage arising from the use of the information contained in this book.

# Contents

# What is Version Control and Why It Matters

## Introduction to Version Control

Version control is the backbone of modern software development. At its core, it's a system that tracks changes to files over time. Think of it as a historian for your code, recording every addition, deletion, and modification. Whether you're a solo developer or part of a large team, version control helps you keep track of your work and collaborate effectively.

Imagine you're writing a book. Without version control, you'd need to create endless copies—*Book_Final*, *Book_Final_v2*, *Book_FINAL_FINAL*. Sound familiar? Version control solves this chaos by letting you save changes in a structured, organized way.

## Overview of Version Control Systems

There are two main types of version control systems: **centralized** and **distributed**.

1. **Centralized Version Control Systems (CVCS):**

   o In a centralized system, all files and their histories are stored on a central server.

   o Developers check out files, make changes, and then check them back in.

   o Example: Subversion (SVN).

   o **Pros**: Simpler setup, single source of truth.

   o **Cons**: If the central server goes down, no one can access the history or collaborate.

2. **Distributed Version Control Systems (DVCS):**

   o Here, every developer has a complete copy of the entire project history on their machine.

   o Changes can be made locally and then shared with others.

   o Example: Git, Mercurial.

   o **Pros**: No single point of failure, faster operations, easy branching.

   o **Cons**: Steeper learning curve.

**Why Git Stands Out:**
Git, the most popular DVCS, has become the industry standard because it's fast, flexible, and works offline.

It also enables collaboration at a scale unimaginable with older systems.

---

# Why Version Control Matters

Version control isn't just about tracking changes—it's about improving your workflow, reducing errors, and enhancing collaboration. Let's explore some of the key benefits:

1. **Backup and Recovery:**
   Mistakes happen. Maybe you delete an important file, or a bug breaks your code. Version control lets you roll back to a previous state with minimal effort.
   **Example:** A developer accidentally deletes a configuration file. Instead of panicking, they use Git to restore the file from the last commit.

2. **Collaboration:**
   In a team, multiple people often work on the same codebase. Version control ensures everyone can work simultaneously without overwriting each other's work.
   **Example:** Two developers, Alice and Bob, are working on different features. Using Git, they each create branches to work independently and merge their changes when ready.

3. **Audit Trail:**
   Version control keeps a record of who changed what and why. This is invaluable for debugging and accountability.

website's CSS file, ensuring they can roll back if a style update causes visual glitches.

---

# How Version Control Fits into the Software Development Lifecycle

1. **Planning:**
   During the planning phase, version control helps teams organize their ideas and create a roadmap.
   **Example:** Creating a repository with a README file outlining the project's goals.

2. **Development:**
   As developers write code, they commit their work regularly, ensuring progress is saved and shared. Branching allows them to work on features independently.

3. **Testing:**
   Version control integrates with testing tools, enabling automated tests to run on every code update.

4. **Deployment:**
   CI/CD pipelines, powered by version control, automate deployments to staging or production environments.

5. **Maintenance:**
   During the maintenance phase, version control helps teams fix bugs and add updates without disrupting the main application.

Version control is more than a tool—it's a mindset. By embracing version control, you're not just tracking your code; you're building a framework for collaboration, experimentation, and growth. Whether you're working solo or as part of a global team, version control is the foundation for managing modern software development.

From fixing bugs to deploying features, the benefits of version control are clear. It empowers developers to work smarter, collaborate better, and deliver high-quality software with confidence. In the next chapter, we'll dive deeper into Git, the most popular version control system, and explore how to get started with it.

# Getting Started with Git

### Introduction

Git is a distributed version control system that's become the gold standard for developers worldwide. It allows you to track changes in your projects, collaborate effectively with others, and experiment without fear of losing progress. In this chapter, we'll guide you through installing Git, setting up your first repository, and creating a personal project. By the end, you'll have a hands-on understanding of how to start using Git effectively.

---

## Installing Git on Different Platforms

Git works across various operating systems. Below, we outline installation instructions for Windows, macOS, and Linux.

### 1. Installing Git on Windows

1. **Download Git:**
   Visit the official Git website at git-scm.com and download the latest version for Windows.

2. **Run the Installer:**
   Open the downloaded .exe file and follow the

installation wizard. Key options to pay attention to:

- ○ Select "Use Git from the command line and also from third-party software" for versatility.

- ○ Choose a text editor (default is Vim; you can opt for Notepad++ or VS Code).

- ○ Leave default options for other settings unless you have specific needs.

3. **Verify Installation:**
   Open the Command Prompt or PowerShell and type:

css

```
git --version
```

If Git is installed correctly, it will display the version number.

## 2. Installing Git on macOS

1. **Use Homebrew (Preferred Method):**
   If Homebrew isn't installed, first install it by running:

bash

```
/bin/bash -c "$(curl -fsSL https://raw.githubusercontent.com/Homebrew/install/HEAD/install.sh)"
```

Then, install Git with:

brew install git

2. **Verify Installation:**
   Open Terminal and type:

css

git --version

3. **Alternative Method:**
   Git may already be installed with Xcode
   Command Line Tools. Check by typing:

css

git --version

If not installed, run:

lua

xcode-select –install

## 3. Installing Git on Linux

1. **Use Your Distribution's Package Manager:**

   o **Ubuntu/Debian:**

sql

```
sudo apt update
sudo apt install git
```

- **Fedora:**

```
sudo dnf install git
```

- **Arch:**

```
sudo pacman -S git
```

2. **Verify Installation:**
   Open the terminal and type:

css

```
git --version
```

---

# Setting Up Your First Repository

Once Git is installed, it's time to set up your first repository—a place where Git will track your files.

## 1. Configuring Git

Before creating a repository, configure Git with your user details. These details will be linked to your commits.

1. Open your terminal and set your name and email:

arduino

git config --global user.name "Your Name"

git config --global user.email "your.email@example.com"

2. Verify your configuration:

lua

git config --list

You should see your name and email listed.

## 2. Creating a Repository

A Git repository (repo) is a project folder tracked by Git.

1. **Initialize a Repository:**
   Choose or create a directory for your project. Navigate to it in the terminal and run:

csharp

git init

This initializes an empty Git repository. Git creates a hidden folder, .git, to store all version history.

2. **Add Files:**
   Add some files to your directory. For example, create a README.md file:

bash

```
echo "# My First Project" > README.md
```

3. **Stage Files:**
   To start tracking changes, stage your file with:

csharp

```
git add README.md
```

Staging tells Git to include this file in the next commit.

4. **Commit Changes:**
   A commit is like a snapshot of your project. Commit your staged file with:

sql

```
git commit -m "Initial commit: Add README"
```

## 3. Verifying Your Repository

1. View the status of your repository:

lua

git status

This command shows which files are staged, modified, or untracked.

2. View commit history:

bash

git log

This lists all commits, starting with the most recent.

---

# Real-World Example: Creating a Personal Project Repository

Let's walk through creating a personal project repository for a simple "To-Do List" application.

### Step 1: Set Up the Project Folder

1. Create a new folder for your project:

bash

mkdir todo-list

cd todo-list

2. Initialize Git in this folder:

csharp

```
git init
```

**Step 2: Create the Initial Files**

1. Add a README.md file with a project description:

bash

```
echo "# To-Do List Application" > README.md
```

2. Create a basic file structure:

bash

```
mkdir src
touch src/index.html src/style.css src/app.js
```

3. Check the status of your repository:

lua

```
git status
```

**Step 3: Stage and Commit Changes**

1. Stage all files:

csharp

```
git add .
```

The . stages all changes in the directory.

2. Commit your changes:

sql

```
git commit -m "Initial commit: Set up project structure"
```

**Step 4: Connect to a Remote Repository**

To share your project or collaborate, connect it to a remote repository, such as GitHub.

1. **Create a Repository on GitHub:**

   - Go to GitHub and log in.

   - Click "New Repository" and name it todo-list.

   - Copy the repository's URL (e.g., https://github.com/your-username/todo-list.git).

2. **Link Your Local Repository to GitHub:**

csharp

```
git remote add origin https://github.com/your-username/todo-list.git
```

3. **Push Your Code to GitHub:**

css

```
git branch -M main
git push -u origin main
```

Your code is now live on GitHub!

---

## Common Pitfalls and Solutions

1. **"Command Not Found" Error:**
    - Ensure Git is installed and added to your system's PATH.
    - Revisit the installation steps for your platform.

2. **Permission Issues with GitHub:**
    - If you encounter permission errors when pushing, check your SSH key or GitHub token.
    - Generate and add an SSH key:

css

```
ssh-keygen -t rsa -b 4096 -C "your.email@example.com"
```

3. **Forgot to Stage Files Before Commit:**
    - If you forget to stage changes, you can stage and commit them after the fact:

sql

```
git add .
```

```
git commit -m "Add forgotten changes"
```

---

Congratulations! You've taken the first steps into the world of Git. Installing Git, configuring it, and creating your first repository are foundational skills every developer needs. With this setup, you're ready to manage your code, experiment with new ideas, and collaborate with others.

In the next chapter, we'll explore **core Git concepts**, such as the working directory, staging area, and commits, to deepen your understanding of how Git operates under the hood.

# Core Concepts of Git

## Introduction

To use Git effectively, you need to understand its core concepts and how it organizes your work. At the heart of Git are the **Working Directory**, **Staging Area**, and **Repository**. These three areas represent different stages of your project and changes. In this chapter, we'll break these concepts down and introduce the idea of **snapshots vs. deltas**, helping you understand how Git records changes. By the end, you'll know how to make your first commit and grasp the process behind it.

---

# Working Directory, Staging Area, and Repository

Git uses a three-step workflow to track changes, giving you flexibility and control over your project.

### 1. Working Directory

The working directory is the folder on your computer where your project files live. It's the workspace where you make changes to your code or other files.

- **Example:**
  Imagine you're working on a to-do list project. The src folder containing index.html, style.css, and app.js represents your working directory.

**Key Points:**

- Any file you create, edit, or delete in this directory is considered **modified**.

- Git keeps track of these changes but doesn't automatically save them to the history.

## 2. Staging Area

The staging area is a place where you prepare files for a commit. Think of it as a waiting room for changes you want to save.

- **Example:**
  If you update style.css to add a new background color, you can stage this specific change to be included in your next snapshot.

**Commands:**

- git add <file>: Adds a file to the staging area.

- git status: Shows which files are staged or still modified.

**Why It's Useful:** The staging area allows you to organize your commits by choosing only the changes you want to include. This is helpful for creating meaningful, atomic commits (small, focused changes).

## 3. Repository

The repository is the database where Git stores your project's entire history. It includes every commit you've made and their associated metadata.

- **Example:**
  After committing changes to style.css, the repository saves a snapshot of that file at that point in time.

**Types of Repositories:**

- **Local Repository:** Lives on your computer and tracks changes only you make.

- **Remote Repository:** Lives on a server (e.g., GitHub) and can be shared with others.

---

# Snapshots vs. Deltas

Understanding how Git tracks changes is critical for grasping its power and efficiency.

### 1. Snapshots

Git doesn't just record the differences (deltas) between file versions—it takes **snapshots** of the entire project at the time of each commit. However, it optimizes storage by reusing unchanged files between snapshots.

- **Analogy:**
  Imagine taking a photo of your workspace each time you finish a task. Each photo captures the full state of your desk but only saves changes (like a new piece of paper) to save space.

### 2. Deltas (Used by Older Systems)

Traditional version control systems, like Subversion, store only the differences (deltas) between file versions. While this can save storage space, it makes certain operations (like reviewing file history) slower because the system must reconstruct past versions by applying deltas sequentially.

**Why Snapshots Matter**

Git's snapshot-based model makes operations like branching, merging, and rollbacks much faster because every commit represents a complete state of your project.

---

# Making Your First Commit and Understanding the Process

Let's go through the process of making your first commit step by step with an example project.

### Step 1: Set Up a Project

1. Create a new folder for your project:

perl

```
mkdir my-first-git-project
cd my-first-git-project
```

2. Initialize a Git repository:

csharp

git init

Output:

sql

Initialized empty Git repository in /path/to/my-first-git-project/.git/

**Step 2: Create and Modify Files**

    1.  Add a file to your project:

bash

```
echo "Hello, Git!" > hello.txt
```

    2.  Check the status of your repository:

lua

```
git status
```

Output:

makefile

Untracked files:

  (use "git add <file>..." to include in what will be committed)

    hello.txt

### Step 3: Stage Changes

Staging tells Git which files to include in the next commit.

    1.  Add hello.txt to the staging area:

csharp

```
git add hello.txt
```

    2.  Check the status again:

lua

```
git status
```

Output:

vbnet

```
Changes to be committed:
  (use "git restore --staged <file>..." to unstage)
    new file:   hello.txt
```

### Step 4: Commit Changes

A commit saves a snapshot of the staged changes to your repository.

    1.  Commit your staged changes:

sql

git commit -m "Initial commit: Add hello.txt"

Output:

sql

[main (root-commit) 1a2b3c4] Initial commit: Add hello.txt

 1 file changed, 1 insertion(+)

 create mode 100644 hello.txt

**Step 5: View Commit History**

Review the history of your commits:

bash

git log

Output:

sql

commit 1a2b3c4 (HEAD -> main)

Author: Your Name <your.email@example.com>

Date:   YYYY-MM-DD HH:MM:SS

  Initial commit: Add hello.txt

# Visualizing the Process

Here's a simple flowchart of what happens during these steps:

1. **Working Directory:**
   - You create or modify files (e.g., hello.txt).

2. **Staging Area:**
   - Use git add to stage changes.
   - Staged files are marked for inclusion in the next commit.

3. **Repository:**
   - Use git commit to save a snapshot of the staged changes.
   - The repository updates to include this new snapshot.

---

# Common Pitfalls and Solutions

1. **Forgetting to Stage Files:**
   If you forget to stage a file, Git won't include it in the commit.

   - Solution: Use git add <file> or git add . to stage all changes.

2. **Accidentally Committing Unintended Changes:**
   If you stage and commit a file by mistake:

   ○ Undo the commit (but keep changes):

perl

git reset HEAD~

   ○ This moves the commit's changes back to the staging area.

3. **Committing Without a Message:**
   If you run git commit without -m, Git will open your default editor for you to write a message.

   ○ Solution: Close the editor if this happens by mistake, and run the command again with -m.

# Practical Exercise

Try this simple exercise to reinforce your understanding:

1. Create a project folder and initialize a Git repository.

2. Create three files: file1.txt, file2.txt, and file3.txt.

3. Stage and commit only file1.txt with a meaningful message.

4.  Modify file2.txt and file3.txt, stage them, and commit them together.

5.  Check your commit history and verify that each commit only includes the intended changes.

---

The concepts of the working directory, staging area, and repository form the foundation of Git's workflow. Understanding snapshots vs. deltas clarifies why Git is both powerful and efficient. By practicing the process of staging and committing changes, you're well on your way to mastering version control.

In the next chapter, we'll build on these concepts and explore **basic Git commands** like status, log, and diff to help you navigate your repository and troubleshoot common issues.

# Basic Git Commands

### Introduction

Understanding Git's fundamental commands is essential for effective version control. In this chapter, we'll cover the most frequently used commands: git init, git add, git commit, git status, and git log. Each command serves a distinct purpose in Git's workflow. Along the way, we'll go through a hands-on walkthrough to reinforce your understanding.

---

## 1. git init – Initialize a Repository

The git init command initializes a new Git repository. It creates a hidden .git folder in your project directory, where Git stores all its metadata and history.

### Syntax

csharp

```
git init
```

### Use Case

When you start a new project, you use git init to turn the folder into a Git repository.

### Example

1. Create a new directory:

perl

```
mkdir my-first-repo
cd my-first-repo
```

2. Initialize a Git repository:

csharp

```
git init
```

Output:

sql

```
Initialized empty Git repository in /path/to/my-first-repo/.git/
```

3. Check for the .git folder:

bash

```
ls -a
```

You'll see the hidden .git directory, indicating Git is tracking this folder.

---

# 2. git add – Stage Changes

The git add command stages changes, preparing them for a commit. You can stage specific files or all changes in the directory.

**Syntax**

sql

```
git add <file>      # Stage a specific file

git add .           # Stage all changes in the current
directory
```

**Use Case**

After making changes to your files, you use git add to include those changes in the next commit.

**Example**

1. Create a file:

bash

```
echo "Hello, Git!" > hello.txt
```

2. Stage the file:

csharp

```
git add hello.txt
```

3. Verify staging:

lua

git status

Output:

vbnet

Changes to be committed:

   new file:   hello.txt

---

# 3. git commit – Save a Snapshot

The git commit command creates a snapshot of the staged changes. Each commit is stored in the repository with a unique identifier and metadata, including the author, date, and message.

**Syntax**

sql

git commit -m "Your commit message"

**Use Case**

You commit changes to save a version of your project. Commit messages should be clear and describe what the changes include.

**Example**

1. Commit the staged file:

sql

git commit -m "Initial commit: Add hello.txt"

Output:

sql

[main (root-commit) abc1234] Initial commit: Add hello.txt

 1 file changed, 1 insertion(+)

 create mode 100644 hello.txt

---

# 4. git status – Check Repository Status

The git status command shows the state of your working directory and staging area. It tells you which files are untracked, modified, or staged for the next commit.

**Syntax**

lua

git status

**Use Case**

You use git status frequently to keep track of changes and know what needs to be staged or committed.

**Example**

1. Check the status after editing a file:

bash

echo "Adding more text." >> hello.txt

git status

Output:

yaml

Changes not staged for commit:

modified:   hello.txt

---

# 5. git log – View Commit History

The git log command shows the history of commits in the repository. Each commit includes its unique ID, author, date, and message.

**Syntax**

bash

git log

## Use Case

You use git log to review previous commits and understand the history of your project.

## Example

1. View the commit history:

bash

```
git log
```

Output:

sql

```
commit abc1234

Author: Your Name <your.email@example.com>

Date:   Mon Dec 25 12:00:00 2023


    Initial commit: Add hello.txt
```

## Advanced Options

- git log --oneline: Shows a concise history with one commit per line.

- git log -p: Displays the differences introduced in each commit.

# Hands-On Walkthrough: Setting Up and Committing Changes

Let's walk through a hands-on project to apply these commands in a real-world scenario.

**Step 1: Create a New Project**

1. Create a folder for your project:

perl

mkdir my-git-project

cd my-git-project

2. Initialize the repository:

csharp

git init

Output:

bash

Initialized empty Git repository in /path/to/my-git-project/.git/

---

**Step 2: Add and Stage Files**

1. Create a README.md file:

bash

echo "# My Git Project" > README.md

    2.  Check the status:

lua

git status

Output:

markdown

Untracked files:

    README.md

    3.  Stage the file:

csharp

git add README.md

    4.  Check the status again:

lua

git status

Output:

vbnet

Changes to be committed:

    new file:   README.md

---

## Step 3: Commit the Changes

    1.  Commit the staged file:

sql

git commit -m "Initial commit: Add README.md"

Output:

sql

[main (root-commit) def5678] Initial commit: Add README.md

 1 file changed, 1 insertion(+)

 create mode 100644 README.md

---

## Step 4: Make Additional Changes

    1.  Create a new file:

bash

echo "console.log('Hello, Git!');" > app.js

2. Stage all changes:

csharp

```
git add .
```

3. Commit the changes:

sql

```
git commit -m "Add app.js"
```

Output:

scss

```
[main def8901] Add app.js
 1 file changed, 1 insertion(+)
 create mode 100644 app.js
```

---

## Step 5: Review the Commit History

1. View the history:

bash

```
git log
```

Output:

sql

commit def8901

Author: Your Name <your.email@example.com>

Date:   Mon Dec 25 12:15:00 2023


    Add app.js


commit def5678

Author: Your Name <your.email@example.com>

Date:   Mon Dec 25 12:00:00 2023


    Initial commit: Add README.md

    2.  View a concise history:

lua

```
git log --oneline
```

Output:

sql

```
def8901 (HEAD -> main) Add app.js
def5678 Initial commit: Add README.md
```

# Best Practices for Using Git Commands

1. **Commit Frequently:**
   Break your work into small, manageable pieces, and commit changes often with clear messages.

2. **Use Meaningful Messages:**
   A commit message should explain why a change was made, not just what was changed.

3. **Check Status Often:**
   Use git status to stay aware of changes in your working directory and staging area.

---

These basic Git commands—git init, git add, git commit, git status, and git log—form the foundation of your Git workflow. Mastering these will help you manage your projects efficiently and keep a clear history of changes.

In the next chapter, we'll explore **branching and merging**, which are powerful tools for managing parallel development and collaboration.

# Part 2: Intermediate Git Operations

# Branching and Merging: The Power of Collaboration

### Introduction

Branching and merging are fundamental features of Git that make it an essential tool for modern software development. Branches allow developers to work on different features, bug fixes, or experiments in isolation without affecting the main project. Merging combines these branches, integrating the work into a unified codebase. In this chapter, we'll explore how branches work, the difference between simple merges and resolving conflicts, and how to apply these concepts in a real-world team scenario.

---

## 1. How and Why to Use Branches

### What is a Branch?

A branch is a separate timeline of your project. By default, every Git repository starts with a single branch, usually named main. Creating new branches lets you diverge from this timeline to work on specific tasks or features without impacting the main branch.

### Why Use Branches?

1. **Isolate Work:**
   Developers can work on features, bug fixes, or experiments independently.

2. **Parallel Development:**
   Teams can work on multiple features simultaneously without stepping on each other's toes.

3. **Safe Experimentation:**
   New ideas can be tested without affecting the stable codebase.

4. **Better Collaboration:**
   Branches simplify collaboration by keeping changes organized and trackable.

**Branching Workflow**

- **Create a Branch:** Start by creating a new branch for your task.

- **Work on the Branch:** Make changes and commit them to this branch.

- **Merge Changes:** Once the work is complete, merge the branch back into the main branch.

---

# 2. Simple Merges vs. Resolving Merge Conflicts

### Merging Branches

Merging integrates changes from one branch into another. This is typically done when the work on a feature branch is complete and ready to be incorporated into the main branch.

**Types of Merges:**

1. **Fast-Forward Merge:**
   If no changes have been made to the main branch since the feature branch was created, Git can simply move the main branch pointer forward to the latest commit in the feature branch.

**Command:**

php

```
git merge <branch_name>
```

Example:
Merging feature-login into main:

css

```
git checkout main
```

```
git merge feature-login
```

2. **Three-Way Merge:**
   If the main branch has diverged (e.g., other commits were added while you were working), Git creates a new commit that combines the changes from both branches.

Example:
Merging with divergent histories:

css

```
git checkout main
```

```
git merge feature-login
```

**Merge Conflicts**

Conflicts occur when Git cannot automatically determine how to merge changes because both branches modified the same lines in a file.

**How to Resolve Conflicts:**

1. **Identify the Conflict:**
   When a conflict occurs, Git pauses the merge and highlights conflicting files.

css

```
CONFLICT (content): Merge conflict in file.txt
```

Run git status to see which files are affected.

2. **Resolve the Conflict Manually:**
   Open the conflicting file and edit it to resolve the conflict. Git marks conflicts with:

css

```
<<<<<<< HEAD
```

Code from the current branch

```
=======
```

Code from the merging branch

>>>>>>> feature-branch

3. **Stage and Commit Resolved Files:**
   After resolving conflicts, stage the files and
   complete the merge:

sql

git add file.txt

git commit -m "Resolve merge conflict in file.txt"

---

# 3. Real-World Example: Feature Branching in a Team

**Scenario:**

A team is building a web application. Developers are
working on different features:

- Alice is implementing a login system (feature-login).

- Bob is adding a shopping cart (feature-cart).

- The main branch holds the stable production code.

---

**Step 1: Branching**

1. Alice creates a branch for the login system:

css

git checkout -b feature-login

2. Bob creates a branch for the shopping cart:

css

git checkout -b feature-cart

---

## Step 2: Development

1. Alice works on feature-login:
   - Adds a login form to index.html.
   - Stages and commits her changes:

sql

git add index.html
git commit -m "Add login form to index.html"

2. Bob works on feature-cart:
   - Adds cart functionality to app.js.
   - Stages and commits his changes:

sql

```
git add app.js

git commit -m "Add shopping cart functionality"
```

---

## Step 3: Merging Alice's Branch

1. Alice finishes her work and merges her changes into main:

css

```
git checkout main

git merge feature-login
```

- o Since there are no conflicts, Git performs a fast-forward merge.
2. The team now sees the login system in the main branch.

---

## Step 4: Resolving Conflicts in Bob's Branch

1. Bob tries to merge feature-cart into main:

css

```
git checkout main

git merge feature-cart
```

- Git detects a conflict because both Alice and Bob modified index.html.

2. Git displays the conflict:

css

CONFLICT (content): Merge conflict in index.html

3. Bob resolves the conflict manually:
   - Opens index.html and edits the conflicting lines.
   - Stages and commits the resolved file:

sql

git add index.html

git commit -m "Resolve merge conflict in index.html"

4. The merge is now complete, and both the login system and shopping cart are in the main branch.

---

## Step 5: Clean Up

After merging, branches can be deleted to keep the repository clean:

git branch -d feature-login

git branch -d feature-cart

# Best Practices for Branching and Merging

1. **Create Small, Focused Branches:**
   Keep branches focused on a single feature or task. This minimizes conflicts and makes merging easier.

2. **Commit Frequently:**
   Make small, incremental commits to track your progress and simplify conflict resolution.

3. **Use Descriptive Branch Names:**
   Use clear names like feature-login or bugfix-123 to indicate the purpose of a branch.

4. **Test Before Merging:**
   Run tests on your branch to ensure changes won't break the main codebase.

5. **Merge Regularly:**
   If multiple developers are working on the same project, merge changes frequently to minimize conflicts.

# Advanced Topics: Managing Complex Merges

1. **Using Rebase to Avoid Merge Commits:**
   Instead of merging, you can rebase your

branch onto the latest main. This rewrites the branch's history to include changes from main.

css

git checkout feature-login

git rebase main

**Caution:** Rebase alters commit history, so use it carefully, especially in shared branches.

2. **Conflict Resolution Tools:**
   Tools like Visual Studio Code, GitKraken, and Meld provide graphical interfaces to simplify conflict resolution.

---

Branching and merging are powerful features that enable teams to collaborate effectively. Branches allow developers to work independently, and merging integrates their work into a unified codebase. While conflicts can arise, understanding how to resolve them ensures smooth collaboration. With these skills, you're equipped to manage even complex team projects confidently.

In the next chapter, we'll explore **undoing changes and rewriting history**, delving into commands like git reset, git revert, and git rebase.

# Undoing Changes and Rewriting History

## Introduction

Mistakes are inevitable in software development. Whether it's an incorrect commit, accidental changes, or a bug introduced into production, Git provides powerful tools to undo or rewrite history. In this chapter, we'll explore git reset, git revert, and git checkout, discuss the dangers of git rebase, and analyze a real-world case study where a bug is fixed without disrupting a team's workflow.

---

## 1. Undoing Changes: git reset, git revert, and git checkout

### git reset

git reset alters the current branch's history by moving the branch pointer and optionally changing the state of the working directory and staging area.

### Use Cases:

- Removing commits from history (local changes only).

- Unstaging files or reverting changes in the working directory.

**Syntax:**

css

git reset [--soft | --mixed | --hard] <commit>

**Options:**

1. **--soft:** Moves the branch pointer but keeps changes staged.

css

git reset --soft HEAD~1

   ○ Removes the last commit but leaves changes staged.

2. **--mixed (default):** Moves the branch pointer and unstages changes.

perl

git reset HEAD~1

   ○ Removes the last commit and moves changes back to the working directory.

3. **--hard:** Moves the branch pointer and discards changes completely.

css

git reset --hard HEAD~1

- o **Dangerous** because changes are permanently deleted.

**Example:**

- Undo the last commit while keeping changes:

css

```
git reset --soft HEAD~1
```

---

**git revert**

git revert creates a new commit that undoes the changes from a specific commit. Unlike git reset, it doesn't rewrite history, making it safer for shared branches.

**Use Cases:**

- Reverting a bug or mistake in a shared branch.
- Keeping the commit history intact.

**Syntax:**

php

```
git revert <commit>
```

**Example:**

- Undo the changes introduced in commit abc123:

git revert abc123

  ○ Git opens your default editor to create a commit message for the revert.

**Benefits:**

- The original commit remains in history.
- Safe for team collaboration.

---

**git checkout**

git checkout switches branches or reverts files to a specific commit.

**Use Cases:**

- Previewing a previous commit or branch.
- Discarding changes in the working directory.

**Syntax:**

php

git checkout <commit> [-- <file>]

**Example:**

- Switch to a previous commit:

git checkout abc123

- Revert a specific file to the last committed state:

lua

```
git checkout -- file.txt
```

---

# 2. The Dangers of git rebase and When to Use It

### What is git rebase?

git rebase re-applies commits from one branch onto another, rewriting the commit history. It moves your branch's commits to a new base commit, creating a cleaner history.

### Syntax:

php

```
git rebase <branch>
```

### Use Cases:

- Linearizing commit history to make it easier to read.

- Incorporating changes from the main branch into a feature branch.

**Example:**

- Rebase a feature branch onto main:

css

```
git checkout feature-branch

git rebase main
```

---

## Why is Rebase Dangerous?

Rebase rewrites history, which can cause significant problems in shared branches.

1. **Loss of Commits:**
   During rebase, commits can be lost if not handled carefully.

2. **Conflict Resolution:**
   Rebasing introduces conflicts that must be resolved interactively.

3. **Collaboration Issues:**
   If other team members are working on the same branch, rebasing creates confusion by changing the commit history.

---

## When to Use Rebase

- **Before Sharing Your Work:**
  Use rebase to clean up your branch history before merging into the main branch.

css

```
git rebase -i HEAD~n
```

- o   The -i (interactive) option lets you
      squash, reorder, or edit commits.

- **In Feature Branches Only:**
  Rebase only private branches to avoid
  disrupting shared workflows.

---

# 3. Case Study: Undoing a Bug Without Affecting Others' Work

**Scenario:**

A development team is working on a web application. A bug is introduced in the main branch after merging a feature branch (feature-login). The team needs to fix the bug without disrupting ongoing work in other feature branches.

---

**Step 1: Identify the Problem**

1. The bug is discovered in production, and the team investigates which commit caused it:

bash

```
git log
```

Output:

sql

commit abc123

Author: Alice

Date:   2023-12-26


   Add login feature

   2. After reviewing the commit, the team
      determines that the bug was introduced in
      abc123.

---

## Step 2: Fix the Bug Using git revert

   1. Revert the buggy commit:


git revert abc123

   2. Git opens the default editor to create a revert
      message. The resulting commit is:

makefile


commit def456

Author: Alice

Date:   2023-12-26

Revert "Add login feature"

3. The bug fix is now in the main branch, while the original commit remains in history for traceability.

---

**Step 3: Share the Fix**

1. Push the changes to the remote repository:

css

git push origin main

2. Other team members pull the updated main branch to continue their work:

css

git pull origin main

---

# Alternative Approach: Temporary Rollback with git reset

If the bug needs immediate attention but isn't ready for a revert commit, the team can temporarily roll back the main branch using git reset.

1. Rollback the branch:

css

```
git reset --hard HEAD~1
```

2. Work on a bugfix branch:

css

```
git checkout -b bugfix-login
```

- Fix the bug, stage changes, and commit.

3. Merge the bugfix branch back into main:

css

```
git checkout main
git merge bugfix-login
```

**Note:** This approach is riskier because it involves rewriting history.

---

# 4. Best Practices for Undoing Changes

1. **Use git revert for Shared Branches:**
   Revert commits instead of resetting to maintain a clear and collaborative history.

2. **Avoid git reset --hard Without Backups:**
   Always double-check the state of your working directory before using --hard.

3. **Communicate with Your Team:**
   Inform teammates about significant changes, especially when rewriting history with git rebase.

4. **Experiment in Feature Branches:**
   Isolate experimental or risky changes in branches to avoid impacting the main branch.

---

Git's tools for undoing changes—git reset, git revert, and git checkout—offer powerful ways to manage mistakes and maintain a clean codebase. While commands like git rebase have their place, they must be used carefully to avoid disrupting team workflows. By applying these tools effectively, you can confidently handle bugs and mistakes while ensuring a seamless development process.

In the next chapter, we'll dive into **working with remote repositories**, exploring how to collaborate with others using git push, git pull, and git fetch.

# Working with Remote Repositories

### Introduction

Remote repositories allow teams to collaborate by storing project files in a central location that everyone can access. This chapter covers key concepts like cloning, fetching, pulling, and pushing changes. We'll also explain the difference between origin and upstream and provide a practical example of connecting to GitHub and sharing a project.

---

## 1. What is a Remote Repository?

A remote repository is a version-controlled codebase hosted on a server or platform (e.g., GitHub, GitLab, Bitbucket). Developers can clone, fetch, pull, and push changes to and from this repository.

**Benefits of Remote Repositories:**

- Centralized collaboration for teams.
- Backup and accessibility from any device.
- Integration with Continuous Integration/Continuous Deployment (CI/CD) pipelines.

---

# 2. Key Commands for Working with Remotes

**Cloning**

The git clone command copies a remote repository to your local machine, including its entire history and branches.

**Syntax:**

bash

```
git clone <repository_url>
```

**Example:**

- Clone a GitHub repository:

bash

```
git clone https://github.com/username/my-project.git
```

- Output:

vbnet

```
Cloning into 'my-project'...
remote: Enumerating objects: 10, done.
remote: Total 10 (delta 0), reused 10 (delta 0)
Receiving objects: 100% (10/10), done.
```

## Fetching

The git fetch command downloads changes from a remote repository but does not integrate them into your local codebase.

**Syntax:**

php

git fetch <remote>

**Example:**

- Fetch updates from origin:

sql

git fetch origin

- Use git log or git diff to inspect fetched changes before merging.

## Pulling

The git pull command fetches changes and immediately merges them into your current branch.

**Syntax:**

php

git pull <remote> <branch>

**Example:**

- Pull updates from the main branch:

css

```
git pull origin main
```

**Pushing**

The git push command uploads your local commits to a remote repository.

**Syntax:**

php

```
git push <remote> <branch>
```

**Example:**

- Push your changes to main:

css

```
git push origin main
```

---

# 3. Understanding origin and upstream

**What is origin?**

- origin is the default name for the remote repository you cloned or connected to initially.

- It refers to the primary remote where you push and pull changes.

**What is upstream?**

- upstream is another remote, often used when contributing to a forked repository.
- It refers to the original repository from which the fork was created.

**Example Workflow with origin and upstream:**

1. Fork a repository on GitHub.
2. Clone your fork (GitHub sets it as origin):

bash

```
git clone https://github.com/your-username/repo.git
```

3. Add the original repository as upstream:

csharp

```
git remote add upstream https://github.com/original-author/repo.git
```

4. Fetch updates from upstream:

sql

```
git fetch upstream
```

5. Merge updates into your fork:

bash

```
git merge upstream/main
```

---

# 4. Example: Connecting to GitHub and Sharing a Project

**Step 1: Create a Repository on GitHub**

1. Log in to your GitHub account.

2. Click on "New Repository" and fill in the details:

   ○ **Repository Name:** my-project.

   ○ **Description:** A simple project to demonstrate Git remotes.

   ○ Check "Add a README file".

3. Click "Create Repository".

---

**Step 2: Clone the Repository Locally**

1. Copy the repository URL from GitHub (HTTPS or SSH).

   ○ HTTPS URL: https://github.com/your-username/my-project.git.

   ○ SSH URL: git@github.com:your-username/my-project.git.

2.  Clone the repository:

bash

```
git clone https://github.com/your-username/my-project.git
```

3.  Navigate to the project directory:

bash

```
cd my-project
```

---

## Step 3: Add Files and Push Changes

1.  Create a new file:

bash

```
echo "Hello, GitHub!" > hello.txt
```

2.  Stage and commit the file:

sql

```
git add hello.txt
git commit -m "Add hello.txt"
```

3.  Push the changes to GitHub:

css

```bash
git push origin main
```

---

## Step 4: Collaborate with a Team

1. Team members clone the repository:

bash

```bash
git clone https://github.com/your-username/my-project.git
```

2. A team member adds a new file:

sql

```sql
echo "Team collaboration!" > team.txt
git add team.txt
git commit -m "Add team.txt"
```

3. Push the changes:

css

```css
git push origin main
```

4. Other members pull the updates:

css

```
git pull origin main
```

---

# 5. Best Practices for Working with Remotes

1. **Use Clear Commit Messages:**
   Help collaborators understand your changes.

2. **Pull Before You Push:**
   Always pull the latest changes to avoid conflicts:

css

```
git pull origin main
```

3. **Resolve Conflicts Locally:**
   If conflicts arise, fix them before pushing:

bash

```
git merge origin/main
```

4. **Use Feature Branches:**
   Develop new features on separate branches and merge them into main after review.

5. **Set Up SSH Keys:**
   Authenticate with SSH for secure and hassle-free interaction:

css

```
ssh-keygen -t rsa -b 4096 -C
"your.email@example.com"
```

---

# 6. Common Issues and Solutions

### Issue 1: Authentication Failed

- **Cause:** Incorrect credentials.
- **Solution:**
  - Use a GitHub token for HTTPS: GitHub Personal Access Tokens.
  - Use SSH for secure access.

### Issue 2: Conflicts During Pull

- **Cause:** Local and remote branches diverged.
- **Solution:**
  - Merge changes manually:

bash

```
git merge origin/main
```

  - Resolve conflicts and commit.

### Issue 3: Force Push Required

- **Cause:** History rewritten (e.g., after a rebase).
- **Solution:**

- Use --force to overwrite the remote branch:

css

```
git push --force
```

- **Warning:** Force pushing can overwrite others' work.

---

Mastering remote repositories unlocks the full power of Git for team collaboration. Commands like clone, fetch, pull, and push help you interact seamlessly with remotes, while understanding origin and upstream ensures smooth workflows. By following best practices and resolving common issues, you can confidently manage projects and share work effectively.

In the next chapter, we'll explore **stashing and cleaning**, focusing on keeping your working directory organized and handling temporary changes.

# Stashing and Cleaning: Keeping Things Tidy

### Introduction

Git provides tools like git stash and git clean to help you manage your working directory efficiently. These commands are especially useful when you need to switch tasks or deal with unnecessary files cluttering your project. In this chapter, we'll explore when and how to use these commands, and we'll work through a practical example where stashing becomes essential.

---

## 1. What is git stash?

### Overview

git stash temporarily saves changes in your working directory and staging area without committing them. This allows you to switch branches or tasks without losing progress. Later, you can retrieve and reapply these stashed changes.

### Key Features:

- Temporarily stores uncommitted changes.

- Saves both tracked and staged files.
- Works across branches.

**Syntax:**

css

git stash [options]

**Common Commands:**

1. **Save a Stash:**

git stash

o Saves changes and resets the working directory.

2. **List Stashes:**

git stash list

o Shows all stashed changes.

3. **Apply a Stash:**

git stash apply

o Reapplies the most recent stash but keeps it in the stash list.

4. **Pop a Stash:**

perl

git stash pop

> ○ Reapplies and removes the most recent stash from the list.

5. **Drop a Stash:**

sql

git stash drop

> ○ Deletes a specific stash.

---

## When to Use git stash

1. **Switching Branches with Uncommitted Changes:**
   If you're working on a feature and need to switch to another branch temporarily, stash your changes to avoid committing incomplete work.

2. **Pausing Work for Urgent Tasks:**
   Use stashing to save progress and focus on high-priority issues without cluttering your commit history.

3. **Experimenting Safely:**
   Stash changes to try something new, knowing you can revert to the stashed state if needed.

---

# 2. What is git clean?

## Overview

git clean removes untracked files and directories from your working directory. It's useful for getting rid of temporary or unnecessary files, like build artifacts or files added accidentally.

## Key Features:

- Cleans up only untracked files.

- Does not affect tracked files or stashes.

## Syntax:

css

git clean [options]

## Common Commands:

1. **Dry Run:**

git clean -n

- o Shows which files and directories would be removed.

2. **Remove Files:**

git clean -f

- o Removes untracked files.

3. **Remove Directories:**

git clean -fd

   - ○ Removes untracked files and directories.

4. **Interactive Mode:**

css

git clean -i

   - ○ Lets you confirm each file or directory before deletion.

---

**When to Use git clean**

1. **Cleaning Build Artifacts:**
   After compiling code, remove generated files like .class or .o to keep your directory clean.

2. **Deleting Unwanted Files:**
   Remove accidentally added files that aren't ignored by .gitignore.

3. **Resetting Your Workspace:**
   Use git clean to return your directory to a pristine state.

---

# 3. Practical Example: Pausing Work to Switch Tasks

**Scenario:**

You're working on a feature branch (feature-ui-improvements) when your team asks you to fix a critical bug in the main branch. You've made uncommitted changes to several files, but you don't want to commit incomplete work.

---

**Step 1: Save Changes with git stash**

1. Check your working directory:

lua

git status

Output:

yaml

Changes not staged for commit:

    modified:  app.js

    modified:  style.css

2. Stash your changes:

git stash

Output:

perl

Saved working directory and index state WIP on
feature-ui-improvements: abc1234 Add initial UI
changes

3. Verify that the changes are stashed:

git stash list

Output:

sql

stash@{0}: WIP on feature-ui-improvements: abc1234
Add initial UI changes

4. Your working directory is now clean:

lua

git status

Output:

vbnet

On branch feature-ui-improvements

nothing to commit, working tree clean

## Step 2: Switch to main and Fix the Bug

1. Switch branches:

css

```
git checkout main
```

2. Fix the bug and commit the changes:

sql

```
echo "Bug fix applied" > fix.txt
git add fix.txt
git commit -m "Fix critical bug"
```

3. Push the changes to the remote repository:

css

```
git push origin main
```

## Step 3: Return to Your Work

1. Switch back to your feature branch:

```
git checkout feature-ui-improvements
```

2. Reapply the stashed changes:

perl

git stash pop

Output:

scss

Auto-merging app.js

Auto-merging style.css

Dropped refs/stash@{0} (1c2d3e4)

3.  Verify that your changes are restored:

lua

git status

Output:

yaml

On branch feature-ui-improvements

Changes not staged for commit:

    modified:   app.js

    modified:   style.css

---

**Step 4: Clean Up with git clean**

1. After completing the feature, remove build artifacts:

git clean -n

Output:

lua

Would remove dist/

Would remove temp.log

2. Delete untracked files and directories:

git clean -fd

Output:

c

Removing dist/

Removing temp.log

---

# 4. Best Practices for Stashing and Cleaning

1. **Name Your Stashes:**
   When working with multiple stashes, use descriptive names for clarity:

perl

```
git stash push -m "UI improvements in progress"
```

2. **Avoid Overusing git stash:**
   Commit frequently in a separate branch rather than stashing repeatedly.

3. **Use git clean with Caution:**
   Always run git clean -n before executing a clean operation to avoid accidental deletions.

4. **Add Temporary Files to .gitignore:**
   Prevent untracked files from cluttering your working directory by listing them in .gitignore.

---

# 5. Common Issues and Solutions

### Issue 1: Forgetting to Apply a Stash

- **Problem:** You stash changes and forget to reapply them later.

- **Solution:** Use git stash list to see all stashes, then apply the relevant one:

kotlin

```
git stash apply stash@{0}
```

## Issue 2: Accidentally Cleaning Important Files

- **Problem:** git clean deletes files you wanted to keep.

- **Solution:** Always run a dry run with git clean -n before performing the clean operation.

## Issue 3: Merge Conflicts During git stash pop

- **Problem:** Conflicts occur when applying a stash.

- **Solution:** Resolve the conflicts manually, then stage and commit the resolved files:

sql

```
git add file.txt

git commit -m "Resolve stash conflict in file.txt"
```

---

git stash and git clean are powerful tools for managing your working directory. Stashing helps you pause work and switch tasks without committing unfinished changes, while cleaning keeps your directory free of unnecessary files. By using these commands effectively, you can maintain a tidy workspace and stay productive.

# Part 3: Mastering GitHub

# Introduction to GitHub

## Introduction

GitHub is a web-based platform that builds upon Git's version control system. It provides tools for collaboration, project management, and code sharing, making it the hub for developers worldwide. This chapter will guide you through setting up a GitHub account, exploring repositories, organizations, and teams, and practical steps like forking and starring repositories.

---

# 1. Setting Up a GitHub Account

### Step 1: Create an Account

1. Visit GitHub's website.

2. Click on **Sign up** in the top-right corner.

3. Fill in your details:

    o **Username:** Choose a unique name (e.g., dev_student).

    o **Email Address:** Provide a valid email for notifications.

o  **Password:** Use a strong, secure password.

4. Complete the CAPTCHA and click **Create account**.

### Step 2: Customize Your Profile

After signing up, personalize your profile to showcase your work and interests:

- **Profile Picture:** Upload a professional or recognizable image.

- **Bio:** Add a short description about your skills or areas of interest.

- **Pinned Repositories:** Highlight key projects.

### Step 3: Verify Your Email

GitHub will send a verification email. Click the link to confirm your account.

### Step 4: Install Git Locally (Optional)

If you haven't already, install Git on your computer to integrate local repositories with GitHub.

---

# 2. Exploring GitHub: Repositories, Organizations, and Teams

### What is a Repository?

A repository is a project folder on GitHub that stores your code, files, and history. It can be public (visible to everyone) or private (accessible only to specific people).

**Key Components of a Repository:**

- **README.md:** A markdown file that introduces the project.

- **Issues:** Track bugs, features, and tasks.

- **Pull Requests:** Propose changes and collaborate on code.

- **Branches:** Allow parallel development.

**Example:**
The repository https://github.com/torvalds/linux contains the Linux kernel source code.

**What is an Organization?**

Organizations are shared accounts where multiple users collaborate on repositories.

**Features:**

- **Teams:** Create groups within an organization (e.g., developers, testers).

- **Permissions:** Manage access levels for members and teams.

**Example:**
The https://github.com/microsoft organization hosts repositories for Microsoft's projects, like Visual Studio Code.


**What is a Team?**

Teams are groups of people within an organization, organized by roles or projects.

**Example Use Case:**

- **Team 1:** Backend Developers.

- **Team 2:** Frontend Developers.
  Each team has specific access to relevant repositories.

---

# 3. Practical Example: Forking and Starring Repositories

### Forking a Repository

Forking creates a personal copy of someone else's repository in your account. This allows you to experiment with the code or contribute changes without affecting the original project.

### Steps to Fork:

1. Find a repository you want to fork, such as https://github.com/octocat/Spoon-Knife.

2. Click the **Fork** button in the top-right corner.

3. GitHub creates a copy of the repository under your account.

**Example Use Case:**

- You fork an open-source project to fix a bug or add a feature.

- After making changes, you submit a **pull request** to propose your improvements to the original repository.

---

### Starring a Repository

Starring is a way to bookmark repositories you find useful or interesting. It also signals to others that the project is noteworthy.

### Steps to Star:

1. Open a repository, such as https://github.com/axios/axios.

2. Click the **Star** button near the top-right corner.

### Example Use Case:

- Star repositories for future reference, like tutorials or libraries you may use later.

---

# 4. Additional Features to Explore

### Issues

GitHub Issues are a way to track bugs, features, and tasks. Each issue can have labels, assignees, and comments.

**Example Workflow:**

1.  A user reports a bug.

2.  Developers discuss and assign the issue.

3.  The issue is resolved and closed after the fix is merged.

**Pull Requests**

Pull requests (PRs) are proposals for changes to a repository. They allow collaborators to review and discuss changes before merging them into the main branch.

**Example Workflow:**

1.  Create a branch for your changes.

2.  Push the branch to GitHub.

3.  Open a pull request.

4.  Discuss and address feedback.

5.  Merge the pull request.

**GitHub Actions**

GitHub Actions automate workflows like testing and deployment. For example, you can set up CI/CD pipelines that run tests every time code is pushed.

# 5. Practical Walkthrough: Contributing to an Open-Source Project

**Scenario:**

You want to contribute to an open-source library by fixing a bug.

---

**Step 1: Fork the Repository**

1. Visit the repository, e.g., https://github.com/octocat/Hello-World.

2. Click **Fork** to create a copy under your account.

---

**Step 2: Clone the Fork**

1. Copy the forked repository's URL from your GitHub account.

2. Clone it to your local machine:

bash

```
git clone https://github.com/your-username/Hello-World.git
```

---

**Step 3: Create a Branch**

1.  Navigate to the project directory:

bash

cd Hello-World

2.  Create and switch to a new branch:

css

git checkout -b bugfix-correct-typo

---

## Step 4: Make Changes

1.  Edit the file with the bug, e.g., README.md.
2.  Stage and commit your changes:

sql

git add README.md

git commit -m "Fix typo in README.md"

---

## Step 5: Push the Branch

1.  Push the branch to your fork:

perl

git push origin bugfix-correct-typo

### Step 6: Open a Pull Request

1. Visit your forked repository on GitHub.

2. Click the **Compare & pull request** button.

3. Fill in the title and description for your pull request.

4. Submit the pull request for review.

### Step 7: Collaborate

- Address any feedback from the maintainers.

- Once approved, the pull request is merged into the original repository.

# 6. Best Practices for Using GitHub

1. **Write Clear Commit Messages:**
   Summarize what changes were made and why.

2. **Be Respectful in Pull Requests:**
   Provide detailed descriptions and address feedback constructively.

3. **Explore GitHub Explore:**
   Discover trending repositories and projects aligned with your interests.

4. **Set Up Notifications:**
   Stay informed about activity on repositories
   you care about.

---

GitHub is more than a code hosting platform—it's a
community where developers collaborate, learn, and
contribute. By setting up an account, exploring
repositories, and understanding concepts like forking
and starring, you're ready to make the most of this
powerful tool. In the next chapter, we'll dive into
**collaborating with GitHub**, including pull requests,
code reviews, and team management.

# Collaborating with GitHub

## Introduction

Collaboration is at the heart of GitHub's platform. Features like pull requests, code reviews, and discussions simplify teamwork and streamline contributions. In this chapter, we'll explore these tools, learn how to manage permissions and contributors, and work through a case study to understand the process of contributing to an open-source project.

---

## 1. Pull Requests: Proposing Changes

### What is a Pull Request?

A pull request (PR) is a proposal to merge changes from one branch into another. It's a collaborative feature where contributors discuss and review the changes before they're incorporated into the codebase.

### Creating a Pull Request

1. **Step 1: Push Changes to a Branch**
   After making changes in a branch, push it to GitHub:

perl

git push origin feature-branch

2. **Step 2: Open a Pull Request**

   - Navigate to the repository on GitHub.

   - Click **Compare & pull request**.

   - Fill in a descriptive title and summary of your changes.

3. **Step 3: Submit for Review**
   Submit the pull request, and it will be visible to maintainers for review.

**Reviewing Pull Requests**

When reviewing PRs, team members can:

- **Leave Comments:** Provide feedback on specific lines of code.

- **Request Changes:** Highlight necessary fixes before merging.

- **Approve the PR:** Signal that the changes are ready for integration.

**Merging Pull Requests**

Once approved, PRs can be merged into the target branch:

- **Merge Commit:** Creates a new commit that combines changes.

- **Squash and Merge:** Combines all commits into one for a cleaner history.

- **Rebase and Merge:** Reapplies commits onto the target branch without creating a merge commit.

---

# 2. Code Reviews: Ensuring Quality

## Why Code Reviews Matter

Code reviews are an essential part of collaborative development, ensuring:

- Code quality and maintainability.

- Catching bugs or design flaws early.

- Sharing knowledge and improving team skills.

## Best Practices for Code Reviews

1. **Be Constructive:** Focus on the code, not the coder.

2. **Ask Questions:** Clarify code logic or design choices.

3. **Provide Alternatives:** Suggest better solutions where applicable.

4. **Check for Style and Standards:** Ensure code adheres to team guidelines.

## Code Review Tools on GitHub

- **Inline Comments:** Comment directly on lines of code.

- **Review Summaries:** Leave an overall review (Approve, Comment, or Request Changes).

- **Draft Pull Requests:** Submit early for feedback while still working.

---

# 3. Discussions: Engaging the Community

**What are Discussions?**

GitHub Discussions are forums within repositories for broader conversations beyond specific code changes. They help:

- Share ideas and gather feedback.

- Discuss implementation approaches.

- Build a sense of community around a project.

**Starting a Discussion**

1. Navigate to the **Discussions** tab in a repository.

2. Click **New Discussion** and choose a category (e.g., Q&A, Ideas, General).

3. Write a clear title and description, then post.

**Example Use Case:**

- A contributor proposes a new feature in Discussions to gauge interest before starting development.

---

# 4. Managing Permissions and Contributors

### Understanding Roles

GitHub allows fine-grained control over access to repositories through roles:

1. **Owner:** Full control, including managing settings and contributors.

2. **Admin:** Manage repository settings and permissions but not delete the repository.

3. **Maintainer:** Review and merge pull requests, manage issues, and assign tasks.

4. **Contributor:** Push changes to non-protected branches, submit pull requests.

5. **Viewer:** Read-only access to the repository.

### Managing Permissions

1. **Step 1: Go to Settings**
   Navigate to the repository and click **Settings > Manage Access**.

2. **Step 2: Add Collaborators**
   Click **Invite a collaborator** and enter their GitHub username.

3.  **Step 3: Set Permissions**
    Choose the appropriate role (Admin, Write, Read, etc.).

---

# 5. Case Study: Contributing to an Open-Source Project

## Scenario

You're contributing to an open-source library for data visualization. You want to fix a bug and submit your changes for review.

---

## Step 1: Find a Repository

Search GitHub for repositories that align with your interests, such as https://github.com/d3/d3 for data visualization.

---

## Step 2: Fork the Repository

1.  Click the **Fork** button to create a copy in your account.

2.  Clone the forked repository:

bash

```
git clone https://github.com/your-username/d3.git
```

```
cd d3
```

---

## Step 3: Create a Branch

1. Create a new branch for your fix:

css

```
git checkout -b bugfix-tooltip
```

---

## Step 4: Fix the Bug

1. Locate the file causing the issue.

2. Make necessary changes and test the fix locally.

3. Stage and commit your changes:

sql

```
git add .
git commit -m "Fix tooltip rendering bug"
```

---

## Step 5: Push Your Changes

1. Push the branch to your fork:

perl

```
git push origin bugfix-tooltip
```

---

## Step 6: Submit a Pull Request

1. Open your forked repository on GitHub.

2. Click **Compare & pull request**.

3. Fill in the PR template, detailing the issue and your fix.

4. Submit the pull request.

---

## Step 7: Collaborate

1. Address any feedback from maintainers.

2. Update the PR with additional commits if necessary:

sql

```
git add .
git commit -m "Refactor tooltip fix based on feedback"
git push
```

---

## Step 8: Merge and Celebrate

Once the PR is approved, the maintainer merges it into the main repository. Your contribution is now part of the project!

---

# 6. Best Practices for Collaboration

1. **Follow Contribution Guidelines:**
   Many repositories have CONTRIBUTING.md files outlining how to contribute.

2. **Communicate Clearly:**
   Provide detailed descriptions in pull requests and reviews.

3. **Be Respectful:**
   Maintain a positive tone in discussions and reviews.

4. **Use Draft PRs for Early Feedback:**
   Submit draft PRs to gather feedback before finalizing changes.

---

# 7. Common Issues and Solutions

### Issue 1: Merge Conflicts

- **Problem:** Conflicts occur during pull requests.

- **Solution:** Fetch the latest changes and resolve conflicts locally:

css

```
git fetch upstream main

git merge upstream/main

git push origin bugfix-tooltip
```

**Issue 2: Lack of Response from Maintainers**

- **Problem:** Your pull request is ignored.

- **Solution:** Gently nudge maintainers by commenting on the PR or joining Discussions.

**Issue 3: Permissions Errors**

- **Problem:** Unable to push changes to a branch.

- **Solution:** Check your permissions and push to a fork instead.

---

Collaborating on GitHub through pull requests, code reviews, and discussions fosters teamwork and innovation. By managing permissions effectively and following best practices, you can contribute meaningfully to any project. In the next chapter, we'll dive into **GitHub Actions and Automation**, exploring how to automate testing, builds, and deployments.

# GitHub Actions and Automation

## Introduction

GitHub Actions is a powerful automation tool that integrates seamlessly with GitHub repositories. It enables developers to create workflows for Continuous Integration and Continuous Deployment (CI/CD) pipelines, automate repetitive tasks, and manage project workflows efficiently. In this chapter, we'll introduce CI/CD pipelines, explore how GitHub Actions automates builds, tests, and deployments, and provide a practical example of creating an automated deployment pipeline.

---

# 1. Introduction to CI/CD Pipelines with GitHub Actions

### What is CI/CD?

- **Continuous Integration (CI):** Automates the testing and integration of code changes into a shared repository. Developers can ensure new code works with existing code.

- **Continuous Deployment (CD):** Automates the delivery of code changes to production or other environments once they pass tests.

**Why Use CI/CD?**

1. Detect bugs early.

2. Streamline development workflows.

3. Ensure consistent deployments.

4. Save time with automation.

**GitHub Actions for CI/CD**

GitHub Actions provides a way to define workflows as code using **YAML files** in the .github/workflows/ directory. These workflows can:

- Build and test code automatically.

- Deploy applications to servers, clouds, or other environments.

- Notify teams about workflow results.

---

# 2. Automating Builds, Tests, and Deployments

**Key Components of GitHub Actions**

1. **Workflow:** A set of steps and jobs defined in a YAML file.

2. **Job:** A group of steps that execute on the same runner (e.g., a build job).

3. **Step:** An individual task, such as running a script or installing dependencies.

4. **Runner:** A server where workflows are executed. GitHub provides hosted runners or allows self-hosted ones.

## Defining a Workflow

Workflows are triggered by events such as:

- **push:** Triggered when code is pushed to a repository.

- **pull_request:** Triggered on pull request creation or updates.

- **schedule:** Triggered on a schedule (e.g., daily builds).

## Example Workflow: Running Tests

1. Create a file in .github/workflows/ called test.yml:

yaml

name: Run Tests

on:
  push:
    branches:
      - main
  pull_request:
    branches:

```yaml
      - main

jobs:
  test:
    runs-on: ubuntu-latest

    steps:
      - name: Checkout code
        uses: actions/checkout@v3

      - name: Set up Node.js
        uses: actions/setup-node@v3
        with:
          node-version: 16

      - name: Install dependencies
        run: npm install

      - name: Run tests
        run: npm test
```

2. **Explanation:**

- o The workflow runs on push and pull_request events targeting the main branch.

- o It installs dependencies and runs tests using Node.js.

---

# 3. Example: Creating an Automated Deployment Pipeline

## Scenario

You have a React application, and you want to automate its deployment to **GitHub Pages** whenever changes are pushed to the main branch.

---

## Step 1: Prepare the Project

1. Ensure the React project has a build script in package.json:

json

```json
"scripts": {

  "start": "react-scripts start",

  "build": "react-scripts build",

  "test": "react-scripts test",

  "eject": "react-scripts eject"
```

}

2.  Install the GitHub Pages package:

css

```
npm install gh-pages --save-dev
```

3.  Add a homepage field to package.json:

json

```
"homepage": "https://your-username.github.io/your-repository-name"
```

---

**Step 2: Create a Deployment Workflow**

1.  Create a file in .github/workflows/ called deploy.yml:

yaml

```
name: Deploy to GitHub Pages

on:
  push:
    branches:
      - main
```

```yaml
jobs:
  deploy:
    runs-on: ubuntu-latest

    steps:
      - name: Checkout code
        uses: actions/checkout@v3

      - name: Set up Node.js
        uses: actions/setup-node@v3
        with:
          node-version: 16

      - name: Install dependencies
        run: npm install

      - name: Build the project
        run: npm run build

      - name: Deploy to GitHub Pages
        uses: peaceiris/actions-gh-pages@v3
        with:
```

```
github_token: ${{ secrets.GITHUB_TOKEN }}
```

```
publish_dir: ./build
```

2. **Explanation:**

   - The workflow runs whenever code is pushed to the main branch.

   - It builds the React app and deploys the build folder to GitHub Pages using the peaceiris/actions-gh-pages action.

---

## Step 3: Verify the Deployment

1. Push changes to the main branch:

sql

```
git add .
```

```
git commit -m "Set up GitHub Pages deployment"
```

```
git push origin main
```

2. Monitor the workflow in the **Actions** tab of your repository.

3. Visit your GitHub Pages URL to see the deployed application:

arduino

```
https://your-username.github.io/your-repository-name
```

---

# 4. Best Practices for GitHub Actions

1. **Use Secrets for Sensitive Data:**
   Store sensitive information (e.g., API keys) in GitHub Secrets. Access them in workflows with ${{ secrets.YOUR_SECRET }}.

2. **Optimize Workflow Triggers:**
   Avoid running workflows unnecessarily by specifying branch filters:

yaml

```yaml
on:
  push:
    branches:
      - main
```

3. **Reuse Workflows:**
   Extract common steps into reusable workflows to reduce duplication.

4. **Test Locally:**
   Use tools like act to test workflows locally before committing them:

perl

```perl
act push
```

5. **Monitor Workflow Performance:**
   Use the **Actions** tab to monitor and debug workflow runs.

---

# 5. Common Issues and Solutions

### Issue 1: Workflow Fails

- **Cause:** Missing dependencies or incorrect paths.

- **Solution:** Check the workflow logs in the **Actions** tab for detailed error messages.

### Issue 2: GitHub Pages Deployment Fails

- **Cause:** Incorrect publish_dir or branch settings.

- **Solution:** Ensure the build directory exists and GitHub Pages is configured to use the correct branch.

### Issue 3: Slow Workflow Execution

- **Cause:** Unoptimized workflows.

- **Solution:** Cache dependencies using actions like actions/cache:

yaml

```
- name: Cache Node.js modules
  uses: actions/cache@v3
```

```yaml
with:

  path: ~/.npm

  key: ${{ runner.os }}-node-${{
hashFiles('**/package-lock.json') }}

  restore-keys: |

    ${{ runner.os }}-node-
```

---

# 6. Advanced Use Cases

### Deploying to AWS or Azure

- Use GitHub Actions to deploy to cloud services like AWS, Azure, or Google Cloud:

yaml

```yaml
- name: Deploy to AWS

  uses: aws-actions/configure-aws-credentials@v2

  with:

    aws-access-key-id: ${{
secrets.AWS_ACCESS_KEY_ID }}

    aws-secret-access-key: ${{
secrets.AWS_SECRET_ACCESS_KEY }}

    aws-region: us-east-1
```

### Running Multi-OS Tests

- Test code on multiple operating systems:

yaml

```yaml
jobs:
  test:
    runs-on: ${{ matrix.os }}
    strategy:
      matrix:
        os: [ubuntu-latest, windows-latest, macos-latest]
```

GitHub Actions empowers developers to automate workflows, saving time and reducing manual errors. Whether running tests, deploying applications, or managing complex CI/CD pipelines, GitHub Actions provides the flexibility to meet any project's needs. By applying these concepts and best practices, you can streamline your development process and focus on building great software.

In the next chapter, we'll explore **GitHub Pages for Documentation**, including hosting project websites and configuring custom domains.

# Using GitHub Pages for Documentation

### Introduction

GitHub Pages is a free service for hosting static websites directly from a GitHub repository. It's an excellent tool for hosting project documentation, personal portfolios, or any static content. This chapter explains how to set up GitHub Pages, configure custom domains, and provides a practical example of deploying a portfolio or documentation site.

---

## 1. Hosting Project Documentation with GitHub Pages

### What is GitHub Pages?

GitHub Pages serves HTML, CSS, and JavaScript files from a repository. It integrates seamlessly with GitHub, making it a popular choice for hosting documentation and websites.

### Features:

1. Free hosting for public repositories.

2. Custom domain support.

3. Automatic deployment from the main branch or a specific folder.

4. Integration with Jekyll for creating static sites.

---

**Step 1: Enable GitHub Pages**

1. Navigate to your repository on GitHub.

2. Go to **Settings > Pages**.

3. Under **Source**, choose the branch (e.g., main) and folder (e.g., /root or /docs) for your site.

4. Save the changes. GitHub generates a URL for your site:

arduino

https://your-username.github.io/repository-name/

---

**Step 2: Add Content to the Repository**

1. Add an index.html file:

html

```
<!DOCTYPE html>

<html>

<head>

  <title>My Documentation</title>
```

```
</head>

<body>

    <h1>Welcome to My Project Documentation</h1>

    <p>This is hosted on GitHub Pages.</p>

</body>

</html>
```

2. Push the file to the main branch:

sql

```
git add index.html

git commit -m "Add initial documentation"

git push origin main
```

3. Visit the GitHub Pages URL to view the site.

---

## Step 3: Use Jekyll for Dynamic Documentation

GitHub Pages supports Jekyll, a static site generator. With Jekyll, you can:

- Use templates for consistent layouts.

- Automatically generate pages from Markdown files.

## Steps to Set Up Jekyll:

1. Add a _config.yml file to configure your site:

yaml

```yaml
title: My Documentation
description: Project documentation hosted on GitHub Pages.
```

2.  Create Markdown files for documentation:

    o   index.md:

markdown

```markdown
# Welcome to My Project
This is a detailed documentation site.
```

    o   about.md:

markdown

```markdown
# About the Project
This project is awesome!
```

3.  Push the files to GitHub. Jekyll automatically generates HTML for these Markdown files.

---

# 2. Configuring Custom Domains

## Why Use a Custom Domain?

Custom domains make your GitHub Pages site more professional and easier to remember. For example:

- Default URL: https://your-username.github.io/your-repository-name/

- Custom URL: https://www.example.com

---

### Step 1: Purchase a Domain

1. Use a domain registrar like Namecheap, Google Domains, or GoDaddy.

2. Choose and purchase your domain (e.g., example.com).

---

### Step 2: Configure DNS Settings

1. Access your domain registrar's DNS settings.

2. Add the following **A records** to point to GitHub's servers:


185.199.108.153

185.199.109.153

185.199.110.153

185.199.111.153

3. (Optional) Add a **CNAME record** to redirect www.example.com to example.com:

makefile

Name: www

Type: CNAME

Value: your-username.github.io

---

### Step 3: Link the Domain in GitHub

1. Navigate to **Settings > Pages** in your repository.

2. Under **Custom Domain**, enter your domain (e.g., example.com) and save.

3. GitHub automatically configures HTTPS for your domain.

---

# 3. Practical Example: Deploying a Portfolio or Documentation Site

## Scenario

You're creating a personal portfolio to showcase your projects and skills. The site will include an introduction, project links, and a contact page.

---

### Step 1: Create a Repository

1. Create a new repository on GitHub:

   - Repository Name: portfolio.

- Description: Personal portfolio site.
- Initialize with a README.md.

---

## Step 2: Add HTML, CSS, and JavaScript

1. Add the following file structure:

bash

```
/portfolio
├── index.html
├── style.css
├── script.js
```

2. Create index.html:

html

```
<!DOCTYPE html>
<html>
<head>
    <title>My Portfolio</title>
    <link rel="stylesheet" href="style.css">
</head>
<body>
    <header>
```

```html
<h1>Welcome to My Portfolio</h1>
<nav>
    <a href="#about">About</a>
    <a href="#projects">Projects</a>
    <a href="#contact">Contact</a>
</nav>
</header>
<section id="about">
    <h2>About Me</h2>
    <p>I am a developer with a passion for creating amazing projects.</p>
</section>
<section id="projects">
    <h2>My Projects</h2>
    <ul>
        <li><a href="https://github.com/username/project1">Project 1</a></li>
        <li><a href="https://github.com/username/project2">Project 2</a></li>
    </ul>
</section>
<section id="contact">
```

```html
      <h2>Contact</h2>
      <p>Email me at: example@example.com</p>
   </section>
</body>
</html>
```

3. Create style.css:

css

```css
body {
   font-family: Arial, sans-serif;
   margin: 0;
   padding: 0;
}
header {
   background: #333;
   color: white;
   padding: 1rem;
   text-align: center;
}
nav a {
   color: white;
   margin: 0 1rem;
```

```css
    text-decoration: none;
}
section {
    padding: 2rem;
}
```

4. Create script.js (optional):

javascript

```javascript
console.log("Welcome to my portfolio site!");
```

---

**Step 3: Deploy to GitHub Pages**

1. Push your files to the main branch:

sql

```sql
git add .
git commit -m "Add portfolio site"
git push origin main
```

2. Enable GitHub Pages:

   ○ Navigate to **Settings > Pages**.

   ○ Select main as the source branch.

   ○ Save changes.

3. View your site at:

arduino

```
https://your-username.github.io/portfolio/
```

---

**Step 4: Add a Custom Domain (Optional)**

1. Purchase a domain (e.g., myportfolio.com).

2. Configure DNS as described earlier.

3. Link the domain in GitHub:

   o Go to **Settings > Pages**.

   o Enter myportfolio.com under **Custom Domain**.

   o Save and verify HTTPS.

---

# 4. Best Practices for GitHub Pages

1. **Use .gitignore for Temporary Files:**
   Exclude build artifacts or sensitive files from the repository.

2. **Test Locally:**
   Test your site using a local server (e.g., Python's http.server):

```
python -m http.server
```

3. **Optimize for Performance:**
   Minify CSS/JavaScript and use optimized images for faster loading.

4. **Integrate with Actions:**
   Automate deployments using GitHub Actions for complex sites.

---

# 5. Common Issues and Solutions

### Issue 1: Site Not Loading

- **Cause:** Misconfigured index.html or source settings.

- **Solution:** Ensure the file is named index.html and the correct branch is selected in **Settings > Pages**.

### Issue 2: HTTPS Not Enabled

- **Cause:** Custom domain incorrectly configured.

- **Solution:** Verify DNS records and enable HTTPS in GitHub Pages settings.

### Issue 3: Slow Site Performance

- **Cause:** Large unoptimized files.

- **Solution:** Use tools like ImageOptim for images and Terser for JavaScript.

---

GitHub Pages is a versatile tool for hosting static sites, from project documentation to personal portfolios. By leveraging its features and integrating custom domains, you can create a professional online presence with minimal effort. In the next chapter, we'll explore **advanced branching strategies**, such as GitFlow and GitHub Flow, to manage complex development workflows.

# Part 4: Advanced Git and GitHub Topics

# Advanced Branching Strategies

## Introduction

Effective branching strategies are crucial for managing complex development workflows, especially in large teams. This chapter explores three popular branching models—GitFlow, GitHub Flow, and Trunk-Based Development—along with guidance on choosing the right strategy for your team. Finally, we'll dive into a practical example of managing releases in a large team.

---

# 1. Overview of Advanced Branching Strategies

### 1.1 GitFlow

GitFlow is a highly structured branching model that uses multiple long-lived branches to manage different stages of development. It's ideal for projects with clearly defined release cycles.

**Branches in GitFlow:**

1. **Main:** Contains stable production-ready code.
2. **Develop:** Serves as the integration branch for new features.

3. **Feature Branches:** Created for individual features and merged into develop.

4. **Release Branches:** Created when preparing for a release; used for final testing and bug fixes.

5. **Hotfix Branches:** Used to address critical issues in the main branch.

**GitFlow Workflow:**

1. Start a new feature:

bash

```
git checkout -b feature/login develop
```

2. Finish the feature:

bash

```
git checkout develop
git merge feature/login
```

3. Prepare for release:

arduino

```
git checkout -b release/1.0 develop
```

4. Deploy and merge:
   - Merge release/1.0 into main and develop:

sql

```
git checkout main

git merge release/1.0

git checkout develop

git merge release/1.0
```

**Advantages:**

- Clear separation of concerns.
- Well-suited for large projects with scheduled releases.

**Disadvantages:**

- Overhead due to multiple branches.
- Complexity increases with frequent releases.

---

### 1.2 GitHub Flow

GitHub Flow is a lightweight branching model designed for continuous delivery. It uses short-lived branches and merges directly into main.

**Branches in GitHub Flow:**

1. **Main:** Always production-ready.
2. **Feature Branches:** Used for new features or bug fixes; merged into main after testing.

**GitHub Flow Workflow:**

1. Create a feature branch:

bash

```
git checkout -b feature/login
```

2. Make changes and push:

sql

```
git add .
git commit -m "Add login feature"
git push origin feature/login
```

3. Open a pull request (PR) on GitHub.
4. Merge the PR into main after approval.

**Advantages:**

- Simple and easy to adopt.
- Supports continuous deployment.

**Disadvantages:**

- Lacks the structure needed for complex projects.
- Merging directly into main requires strict code review and testing.

---

## 1.3 Trunk-Based Development

Trunk-Based Development minimizes branching by having developers commit directly to the main branch or short-lived feature branches. It's optimized for teams practicing continuous integration.

**Branches in Trunk-Based Development:**

1. **Main (Trunk):** Single branch where all development occurs.

2. **Short-Lived Feature Branches:** Optional; created for larger changes but merged quickly.

**Trunk-Based Development Workflow:**

1. Create a feature branch (optional):

bash

```
git checkout -b feature/login
```

2. Make small, incremental commits directly to main:

sql

```
git add .

git commit -m "Refactor login code"

git push origin main
```

**Advantages:**

- Simplifies version control.

- Encourages frequent commits and faster feedback.

**Disadvantages:**

- Potentially unstable main branch.

- Requires robust CI/CD pipelines.

---

# 2. Choosing the Right Strategy for Your Team

**Factors to Consider:**

1. **Team Size:**

   - **Small Teams:** GitHub Flow or Trunk-Based Development works well due to simplicity.

   - **Large Teams:** GitFlow provides better structure and control.

2. **Release Cadence:**

   - **Frequent Releases:** GitHub Flow or Trunk-Based Development supports continuous deployment.

   - **Scheduled Releases:** GitFlow is better for managing long release cycles.

3. **Complexity of the Codebase:**

   - **Simple Projects:** GitHub Flow suffices for straightforward workflows.

- - **Complex Projects:** GitFlow or Trunk-Based Development offers better support for managing dependencies.

4. **CI/CD Maturity:**

   - - Trunk-Based Development requires a mature CI/CD pipeline to ensure stability.

---

# 3. Example: Managing Releases in a Large Team

## Scenario

A large team is developing an e-commerce platform. They have multiple concurrent features and regular monthly releases. The team adopts GitFlow to manage their workflow.

---

## Step 1: Initialize the Workflow

1. Set up the main and develop branches:

css

```
git checkout -b develop main

git push origin main

git push origin develop
```

## Step 2: Start a Feature

1.  Create a feature branch for the login system:

bash

```
git checkout -b feature/login develop
```

2.  Work on the feature and commit changes:

sql

```
git add .
git commit -m "Implement login form"
```

3.  Push the branch:

bash

```
git push origin feature/login
```

---

## Step 3: Merge the Feature

1.  Merge feature/login into develop:

bash

```
git checkout develop
git merge feature/login
```

2. Delete the feature branch:

bash

```
git branch -d feature/login
git push origin --delete feature/login
```

---

## Step 4: Create a Release

1. When ready for a release, create a release branch:

arduino

```
git checkout -b release/1.0 develop
```

2. Fix minor bugs and prepare for deployment:

sql

```
git add .
git commit -m "Fix CSS for login page"
```

---

## Step 5: Finalize the Release

1. Merge the release branch into main:

sql

```
git checkout main
git merge release/1.0
```

2. Tag the release:

perl

```
git tag -a v1.0 -m "Release version 1.0"
git push origin v1.0
```

3. Merge back into develop:

sql

```
git checkout develop
git merge release/1.0
```

4. Delete the release branch:

arduino

```
git branch -d release/1.0
git push origin --delete release/1.0
```

---

### Step 6: Handle Hotfixes

1. If a bug is found in production, create a hotfix branch from main:

css

```
git checkout -b hotfix/fix-login main
```

2. Fix the bug and commit:

sql

```
git add .
git commit -m "Fix login redirect bug"
```

3. Merge the hotfix into main and develop:

bash

```
git checkout main
git merge hotfix/fix-login
git checkout develop
git merge hotfix/fix-login
```

4. Delete the hotfix branch:

bash

```
git branch -d hotfix/fix-login
git push origin --delete hotfix/fix-login
```

# 4. Best Practices for Branching Strategies

1. **Define a Clear Workflow:**
   Document your team's branching strategy to ensure consistency.

2. **Automate Testing and Deployment:**
   Use CI/CD pipelines to maintain stability across branches.

3. **Keep Branches Short-Lived:**
   Avoid long-lived feature branches to reduce merge conflicts.

4. **Use Meaningful Branch Names:**
   Follow a naming convention like:

   - feature/feature-name

   - release/version

   - hotfix/description

---

Choosing the right branching strategy depends on your team's size, workflow complexity, and release cadence. GitFlow provides robust support for structured development, GitHub Flow offers simplicity for frequent deployments, and Trunk-Based Development fosters rapid iteration with minimal branching. By understanding and applying these strategies, your team can manage releases efficiently and collaborate effectively.

In the next chapter, we'll explore **handling large projects with Git LFS**, focusing on managing binaries and large assets in Git repositories.

# Handling Large Projects with Git LFS

## Introduction

Git is efficient at managing source code but struggles with large files like high-resolution images, videos, or datasets. Git Large File Storage (LFS) solves this issue by storing large files outside the main repository while keeping lightweight references in Git. In this chapter, we'll explore Git LFS, learn how to manage binaries and large assets effectively, and work through a real-world example of collaborating on a multimedia project.

---

## 1. Introduction to Git Large File Storage (LFS)

### What is Git LFS?

Git LFS is an open-source Git extension that improves how Git handles large files. Instead of storing large files in the Git repository, LFS replaces them with pointers and stores the actual files in a separate location.

### How Git LFS Works

1. **Pointer Files:**
   LFS replaces large files in the repository with small pointer files. These pointers reference the actual file stored in a dedicated LFS server.

2. **Storage Optimization:**
   LFS reduces the size of the .git directory and improves clone/pull times by downloading large files only when needed.

---

### When to Use Git LFS

1. **Large Binaries:**

   o Examples: Images, videos, and compiled libraries.

2. **Versioned Assets:**

   o Files that need to be version-controlled but are too large for regular Git.

3. **Collaborative Multimedia Projects:**

   o Teams working on graphics, audio, or video projects.

---

# 2. Setting Up Git LFS

### Step 1: Install Git LFS

1. **On macOS:**

```
brew install git-lfs
```

2. **On Linux:**

```
sudo apt install git-lfs
```

3. **On Windows:**
   Download and install Git LFS from the official site.

4. Verify the installation:

css

```
git lfs --version
```

---

## Step 2: Initialize Git LFS in Your Repository

1. Enable Git LFS for your project:

```
git lfs install
```

2. Add file types to LFS tracking. For example, to track .png and .mp4 files:

arduino

```
git lfs track "*.png"
git lfs track "*.mp4"
```

3. Commit the .gitattributes file generated by LFS:

sql

```
git add .gitattributes
git commit -m "Configure LFS for large files"
```

---

# 3. Managing Binaries and Large Assets

## Using Git LFS in a Project

1. Add a large file (e.g., example.png) to the repository:

sql

```
git add example.png
git commit -m "Add example image"
git push origin main
```

> - LFS replaces the large file with a pointer and uploads the actual file to the LFS server.

2. Clone the repository:

bash

```
git clone https://github.com/username/repository.git
```

- o LFS downloads only the pointers initially. The actual files are downloaded when accessed.

---

## Monitoring LFS Usage

Check which files are tracked by LFS:

git lfs ls-files

## Storage Limits

GitHub enforces storage limits for Git LFS:

- Free tier: 1 GB of LFS storage and 1 GB of bandwidth.
- Additional storage and bandwidth can be purchased.

## Excluding Files from LFS

To remove a file from LFS tracking:

1. Stop tracking:

arduino

git lfs untrack "*.png"

2. Commit the changes to .gitattributes:

sql

```
git add .gitattributes

git commit -m "Stop tracking PNG files with LFS"
```

---

# 4. Real-World Example: Collaborating on Multimedia Projects

## Scenario

A design team is collaborating on a video project. The repository contains:

- High-resolution images (.png, .jpg).
- Video files (.mp4).
- Supporting documents (.md, .txt).

---

## Step 1: Set Up the Repository

1. Create a repository for the project:

bash

```
git init multimedia-project

cd multimedia-project
```

2. Initialize Git LFS and track file types:

arduino

```
git lfs install
git lfs track "*.png"
git lfs track "*.mp4"
```

    3.  Add and commit the .gitattributes file:

sql

```
git add .gitattributes
git commit -m "Initialize Git LFS for multimedia files"
```

---

## Step 2: Add Large Files

    1.  Add project files:

sql

```
git add image1.png video1.mp4 README.md
git commit -m "Add project files"
```

    2.  Push the changes to GitHub:

css

```
git push origin main
```

        o  LFS uploads the .png and .mp4 files to GitHub's LFS server.

## Step 3: Collaborate with the Team

    1. A team member clones the repository:

bash

git clone https://github.com/username/multimedia-project.git

    2. They download the actual files when needed:

git pull

## Step 4: Versioning Large Files

    1. Update a video file:

sql

cp updated_video.mp4 video1.mp4

git add video1.mp4

git commit -m "Update video file"

git push origin main

          o LFS creates a new version of video1.mp4, keeping the old version available.

    2. View previous versions:

lua

```
git log -- video1.mp4
```

---

# Step 5: Manage LFS Storage

Monitor LFS storage usage on GitHub under **Settings > Git Large File Storage**.

---

**5. Best Practices for Using Git LFS**

1. **Use LFS for Large, Non-Code Files Only:**
   Avoid tracking frequently changing small files with LFS to reduce overhead.

2. **Clean Up Old Versions:**
   Remove unused LFS objects with:

```
git lfs prune
```

3. **Monitor Storage Usage:**
   Keep track of LFS storage and bandwidth limits on hosting platforms like GitHub.

4. **Combine with .gitignore:**
   Use .gitignore to exclude temporary files from version control.

---

# 6. Common Issues and Solutions

## Issue 1: Exceeding LFS Storage or Bandwidth Limits

- **Cause:** Adding too many large files.
- **Solution:** Purchase additional storage on GitHub or use an external LFS server.

## Issue 2: Missing Files After Cloning

- **Cause:** Files tracked by LFS are not downloaded.
- **Solution:** Run:

git lfs pull

## Issue 3: Accidentally Committed Large Files Without LFS

- **Cause:** Files added before enabling LFS.
- **Solution:** Migrate files to LFS:

arduino

git lfs migrate import --include="*.png,*.mp4"

---

Git LFS is an invaluable tool for managing large files in Git repositories. It simplifies collaboration on multimedia and large-asset projects, ensuring that repositories remain fast and efficient. By implementing LFS best practices, your team can handle large projects with ease and maintain a clean version history.

In the next chapter, we'll explore **integrating GitHub with other tools**, including IDEs, Slack, and project management platforms.

# Integrating GitHub with Other Tools

### Introduction

GitHub integrates seamlessly with various IDEs, code editors, and third-party tools to enhance collaboration, productivity, and project management. In this chapter, we'll explore how GitHub integrates with popular tools like Visual Studio Code (VS Code) and Slack. These integrations allow developers to streamline workflows, manage code repositories, and improve team communication.

---

## 1. Integrating GitHub with IDEs and Code Editors

Modern Integrated Development Environments (IDEs) and code editors, like Visual Studio Code, JetBrains IntelliJ, and Atom, offer built-in or plugin-based GitHub integrations. These integrations simplify Git operations such as cloning, committing, pushing, and creating pull requests directly from the editor.

---

### 1.1 Using GitHub with Visual Studio Code

Visual Studio Code is one of the most popular code editors for developers. It provides excellent Git and GitHub integration through its built-in Git support and extensions.

---

### Step 1: Install Visual Studio Code

1. Download VS Code from the official website.

2. Install it on your system and launch the editor.

---

### Step 2: Set Up Git Integration

1. Ensure Git is installed on your system:

css

git --version

2. Open VS Code and navigate to the **Source Control** view (Ctrl+Shift+G or Cmd+Shift+G on macOS).

3. VS Code will automatically detect your Git configuration and repositories.

---

### Step 3: Install the GitHub Extension

1. Go to the **Extensions** view (Ctrl+Shift+X or Cmd+Shift+X).

2. Search for **GitHub Pull Requests and Issues** by Microsoft.

3. Click **Install**.

---

## Step 4: Authenticate with GitHub

1. Click the **Accounts** icon in the lower-left corner of VS Code.

2. Select **Sign in to GitHub**.

3. Follow the prompts to authenticate and authorize VS Code to access your GitHub account.

---

## Step 5: Clone a Repository

1. Open the Command Palette (Ctrl+Shift+P or Cmd+Shift+P).

2. Type Git: Clone and select the command.

3. Enter the repository URL (e.g., https://github.com/username/repository.git).

4. Choose a local directory to clone the repository.

---

## Step 6: Perform Git Operations

1. Use the **Source Control** view to:

- o Stage changes.
- o Commit files.
- o Push and pull changes.

2. Open the **GitHub Pull Requests and Issues** panel to:

- o View and manage pull requests.
- o Create new pull requests.
- o Comment on or review pull requests.

---

### 1.2 Advanced Features in VS Code

- **Live Share:** Collaborate on code in real-time with team members.

- **CodeLens:** View Git blame information above each line of code.

- **Terminal Integration:** Use the built-in terminal for running Git commands.

---

# 2. Integrating GitHub with Third-Party Tools

Third-party integrations extend GitHub's capabilities to include communication, automation, and project management. Tools like Slack, Trello, and Jira connect GitHub to team workflows, ensuring seamless collaboration.

## 2.1 Using GitHub with Slack

Slack is a popular messaging platform for teams. By integrating GitHub with Slack, teams can stay updated on repository activity and streamline communication.

### Step 1: Install the GitHub App in Slack

1. Open your Slack workspace and go to the **Apps** section.

2. Search for **GitHub** and install the app.

3. Visit the GitHub app page in Slack and click **Add to Slack**.

### Step 2: Connect Your GitHub Account

1. In Slack, type /github signin in any channel or direct message.

2. Follow the prompts to authenticate and authorize Slack to access your GitHub account.

### Step 3: Subscribe to a Repository

1. In Slack, type:

bash

/github subscribe owner/repository

- o Replace owner/repository with your GitHub repository (e.g., username/project).

2. Select which notifications to receive:

- o Pull requests.
- o Issues.
- o Push events.
- o Releases.

---

**Step 4: Automate Workflows** Use Slack commands to interact with GitHub directly:

- **Create Issues:**

bash

/github create issue "Bug: Fix login" "Description of the issue"

- **Unsubscribe from Notifications:**

bash

/github unsubscribe owner/repository

---

**Step 5: Monitor Repository Activity** Repository events like pull request updates, issue creation, and push events will appear in the subscribed Slack channel, keeping the team informed in real-time.

---

## 2.2 Other Third-Party Tools

### 1. Trello:

- Use the GitHub Power-Up in Trello to attach pull requests, branches, and commits to Trello cards.
- Track development progress visually on Kanban boards.

### 2. Jira:

- Link GitHub repositories to Jira issues to track commits, pull requests, and build status.
- Use smart commits to transition Jira issues directly from Git commit messages.

### 3. Zapier:

- Automate GitHub workflows with Zapier integrations:
  - Automatically create Trello cards for new GitHub issues.
  - Notify team members in Slack when a pull request is merged.

---

# 3. Example: GitHub with Visual Studio Code and Slack

**Scenario**

A software development team wants to streamline its workflow by integrating GitHub with VS Code for code management and Slack for communication.

---

**Step 1: Code Management with VS Code**

1. The team clones the repository in VS Code:

bash

```
git clone https://github.com/team/project.git
```

2. Each developer uses the **GitHub Pull Requests and Issues** extension to:

   o Create a feature branch:

bash

```
git checkout -b feature/login
```

   o Implement changes and push the branch:

sql

```
git add .
```

```
git commit -m "Add login feature"
```

```
git push origin feature/login
```

- o Open a pull request directly from VS Code.

3. Code reviews and comments are managed in the **GitHub Pull Requests** panel.

---

## Step 2: Real-Time Communication with Slack

1. The team sets up GitHub notifications in Slack:

   - o Subscribes to the repository in the development channel:

bash

```
/github subscribe team/project
```

   - o Configures notifications for pull requests and issues.

2. When a developer opens a pull request, Slack notifies the team:

css

```
[GitHub] @dev opened a pull request: Add login feature
```

3. Team members discuss the PR in Slack and review it in GitHub.

### Step 3: Automating Tasks

1.  A developer creates a new issue from Slack:

bash

```
/github create issue "Bug: Fix login redirect" "Redirect breaks on mobile devices"
```

2.  Slack posts updates for merged pull requests and closed issues:

css

```
[GitHub] @leaddev merged pull request: Fix login redirect
```

---

# 4. Best Practices for GitHub Integration

1.  **Use Single Sign-On (SSO):**
    Secure GitHub and third-party tool access with centralized authentication.

2.  **Minimize Notification Overload:**
    Configure Slack to receive only critical updates by adjusting subscription settings.

3. **Automate Workflows:**
   Use Zapier or GitHub Actions to reduce manual tasks and improve efficiency.

4. **Encourage Team Adoption:**
   Provide training to ensure all team members can leverage GitHub integrations effectively.

---

# 5. Common Issues and Solutions

### Issue 1: Authentication Errors

- **Cause:** Incorrect GitHub credentials or revoked permissions.

- **Solution:** Re-authenticate with GitHub and verify permissions.

### Issue 2: Too Many Notifications in Slack

- **Cause:** Subscribing to all repository events.

- **Solution:** Use:

bash

```
/github subscribe owner/repository [event_type]
```

   o   Example: pulls, issues, or push.

### Issue 3: Pull Request Workflow Missing in VS Code

- **Cause:** GitHub extension not installed or misconfigured.

- **Solution:** Reinstall the **GitHub Pull Requests and Issues** extension and sign in again.

---

Integrating GitHub with tools like Visual Studio Code and Slack enhances productivity by streamlining code management and communication. With features like real-time notifications, pull request reviews, and automated workflows, teams can focus on building great software. By leveraging these integrations effectively, your team can achieve seamless collaboration and efficient project management.

In the next chapter, we'll dive into **troubleshooting common Git problems**, including resolving merge conflicts, recovering lost commits, and fixing repository issues.

# Part 5: Practical Applications and Problem-Solving

# Troubleshooting Common Git Problems

## Introduction

While Git is a powerful tool, it can sometimes present challenges like merge conflicts, detached HEAD states, or corrupted repositories. Understanding how to troubleshoot these issues is essential for maintaining productivity. This chapter explores common Git problems, their causes, and practical solutions with real-world examples.

---

## 1. Resolving Merge Conflicts

### What are Merge Conflicts?

Merge conflicts occur when Git cannot automatically reconcile differences between branches. This typically happens when two branches modify the same lines in a file or one branch deletes a file that another branch modifies.

---

### Example Scenario: Merge Conflict

A developer named Alice is working on a feature-login branch while Bob modifies the same lines in the main branch. When Alice attempts to merge her branch into main, Git detects a conflict.

---

**Steps to Resolve Merge Conflicts**

1. **Attempt the Merge:**

sql

```
git merge feature-login
```

Output:

sql

```
CONFLICT (content): Merge conflict in app.js
```

Automatic merge failed; fix conflicts and then commit the result.

2. **Identify the Conflicts:** Run git status to list conflicting files:

vbnet

```
On branch main
Unmerged paths:
  (use "git add <file>..." to mark resolution)
    both modified:   app.js
```

3. **Edit the Conflicting File:** Open app.js in a text editor. Git marks conflicts like this:

javascript

```
<<<<<<< HEAD
console.log("Code from main branch");
=======
console.log("Code from feature-login branch");
>>>>>>> feature-login
```

4. **Resolve the Conflict:** Modify the file to combine or choose one version:

javascript

```
console.log("Final merged code");
```

5. **Mark the Conflict as Resolved:**

csharp

```
git add app.js
```

6. **Complete the Merge:**

sql

```
git commit -m "Resolve merge conflict in app.js"
```

### Best Practices for Avoiding Merge Conflicts

- Pull the latest changes from main before starting work:

css

git pull origin main

- Commit and push changes frequently to reduce overlapping work.

- Use feature branches for isolated development.

---

# 2. Fixing Detached HEAD States

### What is a Detached HEAD?

A detached HEAD state occurs when Git checks out a specific commit instead of a branch. Changes made in this state can be lost if not properly saved.

---

### Example Scenario: Detached HEAD

A developer runs:

git checkout abc1234

Git moves the HEAD pointer to the specific commit abc1234, detaching it from any branch.

## Steps to Recover from a Detached HEAD

1. **Identify the Detached State:**

lua

```
git status
```

Output:

```
HEAD detached at abc1234
```

2. **Create a New Branch:** To save work done in the detached state, create a branch:

perl

```
git branch fix-detached-state
git checkout fix-detached-state
```

3. **Continue Work:** The new branch now contains the changes, and you can safely commit and push them.

4. **Reattach to a Branch:** If no changes were made, simply switch back to a branch:

css

```
git checkout main
```

### Preventing Detached HEAD States

- Always check out branches rather than commits:

css

```
git checkout main
```

- Use tags to reference specific points in history:

bash

```
git checkout tags/v1.0
```

# 3. Recovering from Corrupted Repositories

### What is a Corrupted Repository?

Repository corruption can occur due to interrupted operations, disk errors, or manual changes to .git files. Symptoms include missing commits, unresponsive commands, or broken branches.

### Example Scenario: Corrupted Repository

A power outage interrupts a git pull operation, leaving the repository in an inconsistent state.

## Steps to Fix a Corrupted Repository

1. **Diagnose the Problem:** Check the error message. For example:

vbnet

```
fatal: loose object abc1234 is corrupted
```

2. **Run Git Maintenance:** Start by cleaning and verifying the repository:

```
git gc

git fsck
```

- o git gc optimizes the repository by removing unreachable objects.
- o git fsck checks the repository for inconsistencies.

3. **Restore Missing Files:** If specific commits or objects are corrupted, re-fetch them:

sql

```
git fetch --all
```

4. **Reclone the Repository:** If corruption persists, reclone the repository:

bash

```
mv repo repo_backup
```

```
git clone https://github.com/username/repository.git
```

Copy uncommitted changes from the backup folder to the new repository.

---

### Preventing Repository Corruption

- Avoid interrupting Git operations like pull or rebase.
- Regularly back up important repositories.
- Use Git hosting services like GitHub for remote redundancy.

---

# 4. Example-Driven Solutions for Real-World Challenges

### Problem 1: Accidentally Deleted a Branch

### Scenario:
A developer deletes a local branch before pushing it to the remote repository.

### Solution:
1. Find the branch's commit using the reflog:

git reflog

Output:

css

abc1234 (HEAD -> main) Commit message

2. Restore the branch:

css

git checkout -b recovered-branch abc1234

---

**Problem 2: Lost Changes After Reset**

**Scenario:**
A developer runs git reset --hard and loses uncommitted changes.

**Solution:**

1. Check the reflog for recent activity:

git reflog

2. Find the commit containing the lost changes and reset to it:

css

```
git reset --hard abc1234
```

---

## Problem 3: Push Rejected Due to Divergence

### Scenario:
A developer attempts to push but gets an error:

arduino

Updates were rejected because the remote contains work that you do not have locally.

### Solution:

1. Pull the latest changes and reapply local commits:

css

```
git pull --rebase origin main
```

2. Resolve any merge conflicts, then push:

css

```
git push origin main
```

---

# 5. Best Practices for Git Troubleshooting

1. **Understand Git Logs and Reflogs:**
   Use git log and git reflog to track commits and branch movements.

2. **Use Stashes for Temporary Changes:**
   Avoid losing work by stashing uncommitted changes:

git stash

3. **Create Backups:**
   Regularly back up your repository, especially before running destructive commands like reset --hard.

4. **Work Incrementally:**
   Commit small, logical changes frequently to make it easier to identify issues.

---

# 6. Common Issues and Solutions Summary

| Problem | Solution |
|---|---|
| Merge conflict | Edit conflicting files, add, and commit. |

| Problem | Solution |
|---------|----------|
| Detached HEAD | Create a new branch or reattach to an existing branch. |
| Corrupted repository | Run git gc and git fsck, or reclone. |
| Deleted branch | Recover using git reflog and checkout. |
| Push rejected | Pull changes with --rebase and resolve conflicts. |

Git's flexibility and power come with occasional challenges, but most issues can be resolved with the right tools and strategies. By mastering troubleshooting techniques like resolving merge conflicts, handling detached HEAD states, and repairing corrupted repositories, you can work confidently with Git and recover from common pitfalls.

In the next chapter, we'll explore **Git in Teams: Best Practices**, focusing on commit guidelines, branching etiquette, and effective collaboration.

# Git in Teams: Best Practices

## Introduction

Effective use of Git in teams goes beyond the tool itself. It requires clear commit message guidelines, structured workflows for code reviews, and proper branching etiquette. These practices ensure seamless collaboration, particularly in distributed teams. This chapter outlines strategies for improving collaboration and provides an example of how a distributed team can optimize their Git workflow.

---

# 1. Commit Message Guidelines

### Why Commit Messages Matter

Commit messages document the history of a project, making it easier to understand changes, debug issues, and onboard new team members. Clear and consistent commit messages are essential for effective collaboration.

---

### Anatomy of a Good Commit Message

1. **Header (Title):** A concise summary of the change (50 characters max).

2. **Body (Optional):** Detailed explanation of the change, why it was made, and any relevant context (wrapped at 72 characters).

3. **Footer (Optional):** Reference to related issues or pull requests (e.g., "Closes #123").

---

**Example Commit Messages**

1. Fixing a bug:

csharp

Fix login validation bug

Adjusted the regex for email validation to support new domains.

This resolves issues users reported with uncommon TLDs.

Closes #45

2. Adding a feature:

sql

Add user profile editing functionality

Implemented a new page for users to update their profile information.

Includes validation for input fields and error messages for invalid inputs.

   3. Refactoring code:

css


Refactor database query methods


Simplified query functions to improve readability and performance.

Added tests to ensure consistent behavior after refactoring.

---

**Best Practices for Commit Messages**

1. **Write in Imperative Mood:**
   Example: "Fix bug" instead of "Fixed bug" or "Fixes bug."

2. **Be Concise but Informative:**
   Avoid generic messages like "Update code" or "Fix stuff."

3. **Use Keywords for Automation:**
   Use terms like "Closes," "Fixes," or "Resolves" to link commits to issues.

# 2. Code Reviews

## Why Code Reviews Are Crucial

Code reviews ensure code quality, foster knowledge sharing, and catch bugs early. They are a cornerstone of collaborative Git workflows.

## Steps for Effective Code Reviews

1. **Prepare the Code for Review:**
   - Ensure the code is tested and adheres to team standards.
   - Write clear pull request (PR) descriptions.

2. **Review Process:**
   - Review the PR for functionality, readability, and adherence to team standards.
   - Leave constructive comments.
   - Approve or request changes.

3. **Merge the Code:**
   - Merge only after all feedback is addressed and approvals are received.

**Pull Request Best Practices**

1. **Write a Detailed Description:**
   Example:

diff

Added feature to allow users to edit their profiles.

- Implemented UI for the profile editing page.

- Added validation for form fields.

- Includes backend API updates.

Test Cases:

- Profile update with valid data.

- Validation errors for empty fields.

2. **Keep PRs Small:**
   Break large changes into multiple PRs to simplify reviews.

3. **Respond Promptly to Feedback:**
   Engage in discussions and address comments quickly.

---

**Reviewer Guidelines**

- **Be Constructive:** Focus on the code, not the coder.

- **Ask Questions:** If something is unclear, ask rather than assume.

- **Suggest Alternatives:** Offer solutions for better implementation.

---

# 3. Branching Etiquette

## Why Branching Matters

A well-structured branching strategy helps teams work on features, bug fixes, and experiments without interfering with the main codebase.

---

## Common Branching Strategies

1. **GitFlow:**

   - Ideal for projects with scheduled releases.

   - Long-lived main and develop branches, with feature and release branches.

2. **GitHub Flow:**

   - Best for continuous deployment.

   - Short-lived feature branches merged directly into main.

3. **Trunk-Based Development:**

   - Suitable for rapid iteration.

- Few or no branches; work happens on main.

---

**Branching Best Practices**

1. **Use Descriptive Branch Names:**
   - Example:
     - feature/user-profile
     - bugfix/login-redirect
     - hotfix/security-patch

2. **Keep Branches Small and Focused:**
   - Limit changes in a branch to a single feature or fix.

3. **Rebase for Clean Histories:**
   - Rebase feature branches onto main to avoid merge conflicts:

bash

```
git fetch origin

git rebase origin/main
```

4. **Delete Merged Branches:**
   - Remove branches after merging to avoid clutter:

bash

```
git branch -d feature/user-profile

git push origin --delete feature/user-profile
```

---

# 4. Example: Improving Collaboration in a Distributed Team

### Scenario

A distributed team is working on a SaaS application with the following goals:

1. Implement a new feature: User profile customization.

2. Fix a critical bug: Login redirection failure.

3. Ensure smooth collaboration across time zones.

---

### Step 1: Define the Workflow

1. Use GitHub Flow for its simplicity and suitability for continuous deployment.

2. Main branches:

   o main for production-ready code.

   o Feature branches for individual tasks.

**Step 2: Assign Work**

1.  Alice starts a feature branch for user profiles:

bash

git checkout -b feature/user-profile

2.  Bob begins a bugfix branch for login redirection:

bash

git checkout -b bugfix/login-redirect

---

**Step 3: Implement Changes**

1.  Alice works on the user profile feature:

    o   Adds the code and commits:

sql

git add .
git commit -m "Add user profile customization feature"
git push origin feature/user-profile

    o   Opens a pull request on GitHub with a detailed description.

2.  Bob fixes the bug:

- Pushes the changes:

sql

```
git add .

git commit -m "Fix login redirection bug"

git push origin bugfix/login-redirect
```

- Opens a pull request referencing the issue:

bash

```
Closes #123
```

---

## Step 4: Review and Merge

1. Team members review the PRs:
   - Provide feedback on GitHub using inline comments.
   - Approve once changes are verified.
2. Merge the PRs into main:

sql

```
git checkout main

git merge feature/user-profile

git merge bugfix/login-redirect
```

---

### Step 5: Deploy and Monitor

1. Deploy the main branch to production.

2. Monitor for issues and address them promptly using hotfix branches if needed.

---

# 5. Best Practices for Teams Using Git

### Commit Best Practices

- Commit frequently to document progress.

- Use descriptive commit messages for traceability.

### Pull Request Best Practices

- Use templates to standardize PR descriptions.

- Require at least one reviewer for every PR.

### Branching Best Practices

- Limit the lifespan of feature branches.

- Regularly rebase branches to avoid conflicts.

---

# 6. Common Challenges and Solutions

**Challenge 1: Merge Conflicts**

- **Solution:** Pull changes frequently and rebase to resolve conflicts early.

**Challenge 2: Poor Commit History**

- **Solution:** Squash commits before merging:

css

```
git rebase -i HEAD~n
```

**Challenge 3: Inconsistent Standards**

- **Solution:** Use pre-commit hooks to enforce coding standards:

sql

```
pre-commit install
```

---

Adopting best practices for commits, code reviews, and branching fosters effective collaboration in Git-based workflows. These strategies ensure that teams—whether local or distributed—can work efficiently, maintain high-quality code, and avoid common pitfalls. By implementing these guidelines, your team can optimize Git workflows and deliver better results.

# Git and GitHub Security Essentials

### Introduction

Security is a critical aspect of using Git and GitHub, especially for teams working on sensitive or high-value projects. Mismanagement of access, credentials, or configurations can expose projects to unauthorized access or malicious activity. This chapter will cover essential practices for securing Git and GitHub, including managing SSH keys, enabling two-factor authentication (2FA), and using token-based access. A real-world example demonstrates how to secure a project effectively.

---

## 1. Managing SSH Keys for Secure Access

### What Are SSH Keys?

SSH (Secure Shell) keys are cryptographic keys that provide a secure and convenient way to authenticate with Git and GitHub. They replace the need for passwords during operations like cloning, pushing, and pulling.

---

## Step 1: Generate an SSH Key

1. Open a terminal and run:

css

```
ssh-keygen -t rsa -b 4096 -C
"your.email@example.com"
```

- -t rsa: Specifies the type of key.
- -b 4096: Sets the key size to 4096 bits for better security.

2. When prompted:

- Enter a file path (or press Enter for the default location).
- Set a passphrase for additional security.

3. Output:

arduino

```
Your identification has been saved in
/home/user/.ssh/id_rsa.

Your public key has been saved in
/home/user/.ssh/id_rsa.pub.
```

---

## Step 2: Add the SSH Key to Your GitHub Account

1. Copy the public key:

bash

```
cat ~/.ssh/id_rsa.pub
```

2. Log in to your GitHub account and navigate to **Settings > SSH and GPG keys**.

3. Click **New SSH Key**, paste the public key, and save.

---

## Step 3: Test the SSH Connection

1. Test your SSH setup:

css

```
ssh -T git@github.com
```

2. Expected output:

vbnet

```
Hi username! You've successfully authenticated, but GitHub does not provide shell access.
```

---

## Best Practices for SSH Key Management

- **Use Unique Keys for Each Device:** Avoid reusing the same key across multiple devices.

- **Use Strong Passphrases:** Protect your private keys with passphrases.

- **Regularly Rotate Keys:** Replace old keys periodically to mitigate compromise risks.

---

# 2. Enabling Two-Factor Authentication (2FA)

### What is Two-Factor Authentication?

2FA adds an extra layer of security by requiring a second verification step—usually a code from a mobile app or hardware token—in addition to your password.

---

### Step 1: Enable 2FA on GitHub

1. Go to **Settings > Security > Two-factor authentication**.

2. Click **Enable two-factor authentication**.

3. Choose an authentication method:

   - **Authenticator App (Recommended):** Use apps like Google Authenticator or Authy.

   - **SMS (Less Secure):** Receive codes via text message.

4. Follow the instructions to configure 2FA.

### Step 2: Backup Recovery Codes

1.  GitHub provides recovery codes to regain access if you lose your 2FA device.

2.  Save these codes securely (e.g., in a password manager or encrypted file).

### Best Practices for 2FA

-   Use a secure and reliable authenticator app.

-   Regularly review and update your recovery codes.

-   Avoid SMS-based 2FA for sensitive accounts due to SIM-swapping vulnerabilities.

# 3. Using Token-Based Access

### What Are Personal Access Tokens?

Personal Access Tokens (PATs) are used to authenticate with GitHub's API and for operations that require account-level permissions. They are safer than passwords for script and programmatic access.

### Step 1: Generate a Personal Access Token

1.  Go to **Settings > Developer Settings > Personal Access Tokens**.

2. Click **Generate new token**.

3. Choose a name, expiration date, and required scopes:

   - **repo:** Full control over repositories.

   - **read:org:** Access organization membership information.

   - **workflow:** Manage GitHub Actions workflows.

4. Generate and copy the token.

---

**Step 2: Use the Token**

1. Replace your password with the token when prompted during operations like git clone:

bash

git clone https://github.com/username/repository.git

When prompted for a password, enter the token instead.

---

**Best Practices for Tokens**

- Use tokens with limited scopes to minimize access.

- Set expiration dates for tokens and regenerate them as needed.

- Revoke tokens immediately if they are exposed.

---

# 4. Real-World Example: Securing a Project from Unauthorized Access

### Scenario

A development team is working on a proprietary software project. The repository must be secured to prevent unauthorized access, especially since some team members are contractors.

---

### Step 1: Enforce 2FA for Team Members

1. Require all team members to enable 2FA:

   - Go to the organization's **Settings > Security > Two-factor authentication**.

   - Enable the **Require two-factor authentication** option.

2. Notify team members to set up 2FA and ensure compliance.

---

### Step 2: Use SSH for Secure Access

1. Require team members to use SSH keys for repository access:

- o Add SSH keys to each member's GitHub account.

- o Remove any saved HTTPS credentials from local Git configurations:

bash

git credential-cache exit

---

## Step 3: Use Least Privilege Access

1. Assign roles based on responsibility:

   - o Admins: Full control over the repository.

   - o Developers: Write access for pushing changes.

   - o Contractors: Read-only access to review code.

2. Manage permissions via **Settings > Manage Access**:

   - o Add users and assign appropriate roles.

---

## Step 4: Audit Access and Logs

1. Periodically review repository collaborators and their roles:

   - o Remove inactive members or those no longer part of the project.

2. Monitor activity using GitHub's **Audit Log**:

   ○ Track changes to settings, permissions, and security configurations.

---

## Step 5: Protect Sensitive Data

1. Use .gitignore to exclude sensitive files:

bash

```
*.env
config/secrets.json
```

2. Use GitHub Secrets to store sensitive variables for workflows:

   ○ Go to **Settings > Secrets and variables > Actions**.

   ○ Add secrets like API_KEY or DATABASE_URL.

---

## Step 6: Enable Branch Protection Rules

1. Protect critical branches (e.g., main) from unauthorized changes:

   ○ Go to **Settings > Branches > Branch Protection Rules**.

   ○ Enable rules like:

- Require pull request reviews before merging.
- Require status checks to pass before merging.
- Restrict who can push to the branch.

---

# 5. Best Practices for GitHub Security

**Repository Security**

1. Set repositories to private unless public access is necessary.
2. Regularly audit repository permissions.

**Credential Management**

1. Avoid storing credentials in the repository.
2. Use encrypted storage for secrets in CI/CD workflows.

**Monitoring and Alerts**

1. Enable Dependabot for automated security updates:
   - Go to **Settings > Security & Analysis > Dependabot Alerts**.
2. Monitor security alerts and resolve vulnerabilities promptly.

**Incident Response**

1. If a token or SSH key is compromised:

   - Revoke it immediately in GitHub settings.

   - Rotate credentials and update configurations.

---

# 6. Common Issues and Solutions

## Issue 1: SSH Authentication Fails

- **Cause:** Incorrect key configuration or missing key.

- **Solution:** Verify the SSH key is added to the agent:

javascript

```
ssh-add ~/.ssh/id_rsa
```

## Issue 2: Token Expired

- **Cause:** PAT expiration.

- **Solution:** Generate a new token and update scripts or workflows.

## Issue 3: Unauthorized Push

- **Cause:** Missing branch protection.

- **Solution:** Enable branch protection rules to prevent unauthorized changes.

---

Securing Git and GitHub is essential for protecting sensitive code and maintaining the integrity of projects. By managing SSH keys, enforcing two-factor authentication, and using token-based access, teams can minimize vulnerabilities and enhance security. Implementing best practices like role-based permissions, branch protection, and regular audits ensures that repositories remain safe from unauthorized access.

# Scaling with Git and GitHub

## Introduction

As projects and teams grow, managing repositories and workflows efficiently becomes crucial. Scaling Git and GitHub for enterprise-level projects involves addressing challenges like large codebases, distributed teams, and multi-repository dependencies. In this chapter, we'll explore best practices for scaling workflows and managing repositories in large organizations, with a case study demonstrating these principles in action.

---

## 1. Challenges in Scaling Git and GitHub Workflows

### 1.1 Large Codebases

- **Problem:** Managing large, monolithic repositories can slow down operations like cloning, pulling, or merging.

- **Solution:** Split monolithic repositories into microservices or use tools like Git Large File Storage (LFS) for handling binaries.

---

## 1.2 Distributed Teams

- **Problem:** Collaborating across time zones introduces delays and conflicts in workflows.

- **Solution:** Implement clear branching strategies and automate integration workflows using GitHub Actions.

---

## 1.3 Multi-Repository Dependencies

- **Problem:** Coordinating changes across multiple repositories can lead to mismatched versions or broken dependencies.

- **Solution:** Use tools like Git Submodules or GitHub Actions to synchronize repositories.

---

## 1.4 Access Control and Security

- **Problem:** Ensuring proper permissions across a large number of contributors is complex.

- **Solution:** Adopt role-based access control, enforce two-factor authentication (2FA), and use GitHub's organization-level settings for consistency.

---

# 2. Scaling Workflows for Enterprise Projects

## 2.1 Repository Management

1. **Monorepo vs. Multirepo:**

   - **Monorepo:** Single repository for all code. Easier to maintain consistency but harder to scale.

   - **Multirepo:** Separate repositories for different services or components. Easier to scale but requires coordination tools.

2. **Repository Naming Conventions:**
   Use consistent naming for clarity:

   - Example:

     - frontend-ui for the user interface.

     - backend-auth for authentication microservices.

3. **Archiving Old Repositories:**
   Archive inactive repositories to reduce clutter while preserving history.

---

## 2.2 Branching Strategies

1. **GitFlow for Structured Development:**

   - Ideal for projects with scheduled releases.

o   Separate branches for features, releases, and hotfixes.

2. **GitHub Flow for Continuous Deployment:**

   o   Simple and effective for teams practicing CI/CD.

   o   Short-lived feature branches merged directly into main.

3. **Trunk-Based Development for Rapid Iteration:**

   o   Few or no branches.

   o   Frequent commits to main with automated testing.

---

## 2.3 Automating Workflows with GitHub Actions

1. **CI/CD Pipelines:**
   Automate builds, tests, and deployments:

yaml

```
name: CI/CD Pipeline
on:
 push:
  branches:
   - main
jobs:
```

```yaml
  build-and-test:
    runs-on: ubuntu-latest
    steps:
      - uses: actions/checkout@v3
      - name: Set up Node.js
        uses: actions/setup-node@v3
        with:
          node-version: 16
      - run: npm install
      - run: npm test
```

2. **Repository Synchronization:**
   Use actions to keep dependent repositories up
   to date:

yaml

```yaml
name: Sync Repositories
on:
  push:
    branches:
      - main
jobs:
  sync:
    runs-on: ubuntu-latest
```

```yaml
steps:
  - name: Sync Repositories
    uses: some/sync-action@v1
    with:
      target_repo: "organization/dependency-repo"
```

3. **Notification Workflows:**
   Notify teams of changes via Slack or email:

yaml

```yaml
name: Notify Team
on:
  push:
    branches:
      - main
jobs:
  notify:
    runs-on: ubuntu-latest
    steps:
      - name: Send Slack Notification
        uses: slackapi/slack-github-action@v1.18
        with:
          slack-token: ${{ secrets.SLACK_TOKEN }}
```

channel-id: "C123456"

text: "Changes pushed to main branch"

---

## 2.4 Role-Based Access Control

1. **Organization Roles:**

   - **Owner:** Full access to repositories and settings.

   - **Admin:** Manage repository settings and permissions.

   - **Maintainer:** Review and merge pull requests.

   - **Contributor:** Push to specific branches.

   - **Viewer:** Read-only access.

2. **Team-Based Permissions:**
   Organize contributors into teams with shared access:

   - Example:

     - frontend-team with access to frontend-ui repo.

     - backend-team with access to backend-auth repo.

3. **Enforcing 2FA:**
   Require two-factor authentication for all contributors to enhance security.

---

# 3. Case Study: Managing Repositories in a Large Organization

**Scenario**

A global e-commerce company is developing and maintaining a platform with the following components:

1. **Frontend UI:** User interface built with React.

2. **Backend Services:** Microservices for authentication, payments, and order management.

3. **Mobile App:** Native app for iOS and Android.

---

**Step 1: Repository Organization**

1. **Separate Repositories:**

   o frontend-ui for the React app.

   o backend-auth for authentication services.

   o backend-payments for payment processing.

   o mobile-app for the mobile platform.

2. **Standardized README Files:**
   Each repository includes:

   o Project description.

   o Setup instructions.

- Contribution guidelines.

---

**Step 2: Workflow Implementation**

1. **Branching Strategy:**
   Adopt GitHub Flow:

   - Feature branches for new functionality.

   - Direct merges into main after approval and testing.

2. **Automated CI/CD:**
   Use GitHub Actions to automate builds and tests:

yaml

```yaml
name: CI/CD Pipeline
on:
  push:
    branches:
      - main
jobs:
  test:
    runs-on: ubuntu-latest
    steps:
      - uses: actions/checkout@v3
```

- run: npm install

- run: npm test

3. **Code Reviews:**
   Require at least one reviewer for every pull request:

   o   Enable in **Settings > Branches > Branch Protection Rules**.

---

**Step 3: Synchronizing Multi-Repository Changes**

1. **Dependency Management:**
   Use Git Submodules to link repositories:

csharp

```
git submodule add
https://github.com/company/backend-auth backend-auth

git submodule add
https://github.com/company/backend-payments backend-payments
```

2. **Version Control:**
   Tag releases across repositories for synchronization:

perl

```
git tag -a v1.0 -m "Release version 1.0"
```

git push origin v1.0

---

## Step 4: Role-Based Access Control

1. **Teams and Permissions:**

    - frontend-team: Write access to frontend-ui.

    - backend-team: Write access to backend-auth and backend-payments.

    - mobile-team: Write access to mobile-app.

2. **Branch Protection:**
   Protect main branches:

    - Require pull request reviews.

    - Enforce status checks.

    - Restrict push access to maintainers.

---

## Step 5: Security and Monitoring

1. **Enable Dependabot:**
   Automatically detect vulnerabilities in dependencies:

    - Go to **Settings > Security & Analysis > Dependabot Alerts**.

2. **Monitor Repository Activity:**
   Use the Audit Log to track changes:

- ○ Go to **Settings > Security > Audit Log**.

3. **Regular Access Audits:**
   Periodically review team permissions and remove inactive contributors.

---

# 4. Best Practices for Scaling Git and GitHub

1. **Adopt Consistent Workflows:**
   Use standard branching strategies and automation to streamline processes.

2. **Automate Everything:**
   Leverage GitHub Actions for testing, deployment, and synchronization.

3. **Use Advanced Features:**

   - ○ GitHub Projects for task management.

   - ○ GitHub Codespaces for development in the cloud.

4. **Prioritize Security:**

   - ○ Require 2FA.

   - ○ Use encrypted secrets in workflows.

   - ○ Enable branch protection rules.

---

# 5. Common Issues and Solutions

| Issue | Solution |
| --- | --- |
| Slow repository operations | Split monolithic repositories into microservices or optimize with LFS. |
| Coordination across repositories | Use Git Submodules or version tagging for synchronization. |
| Unauthorized access | Enforce 2FA and review access permissions regularly. |
| Merge conflicts due to distributed teams | Pull and rebase frequently, and communicate changes proactively. |

Scaling Git and GitHub for enterprise-level projects requires thoughtful repository organization, robust workflows, and effective team management. By adopting practices like automated CI/CD pipelines, role-based access control, and multi-repository synchronization, large organizations can manage complex projects with ease and maintain a high level of productivity.

# Appendices

## 1. Commonly Used Git Commands Cheat Sheet

| Category | Command | Description |
| --- | --- | --- |
| Setup | git config --global user.name "Name" | Set your Git username. |
| | git config --global user.email "Email" | Set your Git email address. |
| Repository | git init | Initialize a new Git repository. |
| | git clone <URL> | Clone a repository to your local machine. |
| | git remote add origin <URL> | Add a remote repository. |
| Branching | git branch | List branches. |
| | git checkout -b <branch> | Create and switch to a new branch. |

| Category | Command | Description |
| --- | --- | --- |
| | git merge \<branch> | Merge a branch into the current branch. |
| **Staging and Commit** | git status | Show the status of the working directory and staging area. |
| | git add \<file> | Stage changes for commit. |
| | git commit -m "message" | Commit changes with a message. |
| **History** | git log | Show commit history. |
| | git diff | Show changes in the working directory. |
| **Remote Operations** | git fetch | Fetch changes from a remote repository. |
| | git pull | Fetch and merge changes from a remote repository. |
| | git push | Push commits to a remote repository. |
| **Undoing Changes** | git reset --soft \<commit> | Reset the branch pointer and keep changes staged. |

| Category | Command | Description |
| --- | --- | --- |
| | git checkout -- <file> | Discard changes in a file. |
| Tags | git tag -a <tag> -m "message" | Create an annotated tag. |
| | git push origin <tag> | Push a tag to the remote repository. |

---

# 2. Troubleshooting Checklist

**Common Issues**

- **Merge Conflict:**
  - o Identify conflicts using git status.
  - o Edit conflicting files, resolve conflicts, and commit the changes.
- **Detached HEAD:**
  - o Create a new branch to save work: git branch <branch>.
- **Corrupted Repository:**
  - o Run git fsck and git gc.
  - o Reclone the repository if issues persist.
- **Push Rejected:**
  - o Pull the latest changes: git pull --rebase.

- o Resolve conflicts before pushing.
- **Accidentally Deleted a Branch:**
    - o Recover using git reflog and git checkout.

## Preventative Measures

- Commit changes frequently.
- Use descriptive commit messages.
- Regularly pull changes to avoid conflicts.
- Backup critical repositories.

---

# 3. Additional Resources for Learning Git and GitHub

## Beginner-Friendly

- Pro Git by Scott Chacon and Ben Straub: Free online book for mastering Git.
- GitHub's Learning Lab: Interactive tutorials for GitHub workflows.
- Khan Academy's Computer Science Section: For foundational coding skills.

## Intermediate to Advanced

- GitHub Docs: Official GitHub documentation.
- Atlassian Git Tutorials: Comprehensive guides for Git workflows.

- GitOps by Weaveworks: Advanced Git practices for DevOps.

**Community and Courses**

- GitHub Discussions: Join communities to ask questions and share knowledge.

- Coursera: Git and GitHub for Developers courses.

- FreeCodeCamp: Git tutorials for beginners and advanced users.

---

**Real-World Case Studies**

**1. Google: Managing a Large Codebase**

**Challenge:**
Google's monolithic codebase, shared across thousands of developers, posed challenges for version control and scalability.

**Solution:**

- Adopted a custom version control system inspired by Git, called Piper.

- Leveraged Git at smaller project levels for collaboration.

**Takeaway:**
For large organizations, scaling Git workflows requires custom tooling and a well-thought-out branching strategy.

---

## 2. Microsoft: Open-Sourcing .NET

**Challenge:**
Transitioning the .NET framework to an open-source project required Microsoft to adopt GitHub workflows for community contributions.

**Solution:**

- Established clear contribution guidelines and templates.

- Used GitHub Actions for automated testing of pull requests.

- Introduced a triage team to manage issues and PRs efficiently.

**Takeaway:**
Open-source projects thrive with transparency, automation, and a welcoming community.

---

## 3. Shopify: Handling Microservices at Scale

**Challenge:**
Shopify's platform consists of hundreds of microservices, each with its own repository, making dependency management complex.

**Solution:**

- Used a multirepo approach to separate services.

- Implemented CI/CD pipelines for each repository using GitHub Actions.

- Established repository templates to standardize configurations across services.

**Takeaway:**
Microservice architectures benefit from repository isolation, automation, and consistent practices.

---

# 4. Netflix: GitOps for Infrastructure

**Challenge:**
Managing infrastructure as code across global teams required scalable and secure Git workflows.

**Solution:**

- Adopted GitOps principles to manage Kubernetes configurations.

- Used GitHub repositories to track infrastructure changes.

- Automated deployments using GitHub Actions.

**Takeaway:**
GitOps provides a scalable model for managing infrastructure, ensuring traceability and collaboration.

---

# 5. NASA: Collaboration on Open-Source Projects

**Challenge:**
NASA needed a platform for collaborating with external researchers and contributors on scientific tools.

**Solution:**

- Opened repositories for projects like WorldWind and Open MCT.

- Used GitHub's organization features to manage teams and roles.

- Enabled branch protection rules to maintain code quality.

**Takeaway:**
Public repositories with clear governance can foster innovation and community engagement.

www.ingramcontent.com/pod-product-compliance
Lightning Source LLC
La Vergne TN
LVHW051321050326
832903LV00031B/3294